WHAT I WISH I'D KNOWN
WHEN I WAS
SINGLE

JOHN BYTHEWAY

DESERET BOOK
SALT LAKE CITY, UTAH

Library of Congress Cataloging-in-Publication Data

Bytheway, John, 1962-
    What I wish I'd known when I was single : how to do life as a young adult / John Bytheway.
        p.   cm.
    Includes index.
    ISBN 1-57345-540-7 (pbk.)
      1. Christian life—Mormon authors.   2. Young adults—Conduct of life.   3. Young adults—Religious life.   I. Title.
    BX8656.B89   1999
    248.8'4—dc21   99-26302
                                            CIP

Printed in the United States of America   72082-6494

10   9   8   7   6   5   4   3   2   1

PROGRAM

PROGRAM NOTES

You know, there's really nothing like a great book. And what you're about to read is *nothing* like a *great* book, but there are a few good things in here, so don't put it down just yet.

This book is about being *single,* being *young,* and being an *adult.* Or, if you want to string the adjectives together, about being a "single young adult" or "young single adult." Now, we all know that the phrase *young adult* sounds like an oxymoron—you know, one of those word combinations that seem to contradict, like "pretty ugly," "freezer burn," "down escalator," "Liberty Jail," or "Zion's Bank." But you are young, and you are an adult, and that means you're in for some major excitement, and you'll need to make some rather pivotal decisions down the road. You, my young adult friend, are a walking oxymoron.

It seems that once you've left the Young Men's or the Young Women's program, there's not a well-defined path of what you're supposed to do anymore. You knew exactly what happened when you turned twelve or fourteen or sixteen, but now it's not as clear. If you're a young man, you have one more step on the path:

preparing more vigorously for your mission. If you're a young woman, you turn and face the world with many more options. Suddenly you must make decisions about education, marriage, or maybe a mission is something you'd like to do too. You're on your own, and it's your big chance on life's stage. Ready or not, it's time to solo.

It's really kind of exciting, isn't it? Isn't this what you always wanted when you were a teenager: to be on your own, to have your own place, to set your own hours for getting up and going to bed? It's kind of nice. But be aware that once you get comfortable doing life as a solo, everyone, and I mean *everyone*, from your bishop to your grandma, will start asking when you're going to add someone else to your act. You know, get married—change from a solo to a duet. For the young men out there, this is a concern only if you've already served your mission. If you have *not* served a mission and are trying to get better prepared, may I suggest putting this book down and getting *What I Wish I'd Known Before My Mission*, or, if you'd rather hear from a more authoritative source, read Alma 17–22. For you young women out there, keep reading. I believe there are many things within these pages that will be helpful to you.

So what is this book about? At first, it's about going it alone. We'll discuss things you ought to do, precautions you ought to take as you have your moment on stage. Most of the rest of the book is about doing life as a young adult, especially as it concerns the single aspect: getting lined up, calling someone up, showing up, breaking up, getting stood up, wondering what's up, giving up, and starting all over again. Eventually we'll even talk about the "M" word: Yes, my friends, *marriage.* (Be careful—don't let anyone among your young adult friends know that you're reading this book. We all know that when it comes to marriage, it's not cool to appear too eager.) Specifically, we'll try to answer questions like these:

How will I know if I'm in love?

Is falling in love some kind of signal that a relationship is right?

Whom should I marry?

Is there a "one and only" for me?

What if both of us get different answers about whether we should marry?

I know marriage is important, but why is it so urgent?

How can I get over a bad breakup?

What's wrong with me?

What do I do while I'm waiting?

When I was a young single adult wondering about these questions, I was under the impression that there wasn't very much available on these topics from Church leaders. Boy, was I wrong. We have not been left alone. I am deeply and profoundly grateful for the wonderful organization that we often abbreviate and call "the Church." We don't have to rely on uninspired Hollywood writers for direction about dating and courtship (thank heaven). Because of the Church, we have access to solid doctrine, true principles, and sound advice from inspired leaders who are very interested in the welfare of the rising generation. As I went through the premarriage process myself, the counsel I had received ever since I was a deacon saved me from making a lot of mistakes.

I tell you this because I want you to know that I'm going to do a lot of quoting in this book. In fact, just the quotes in this book are worth what you paid for it. (But, of course, as an extra-special bonus, you get my somewhat less profound running commentary in between.) I have learned again and again that I don't know very much. But because of the Lord and his Church, I've heard many talks and read many books by people who do. My hope is that you too will benefit from the wisdom of those who have successfully gone from solo to duet status and have left behind many of their notes for us to use.

Don't go around saying the world owes you a living; the world owes you nothing; it was here first.
–Mark Twain

ON YOUR OWN

The powerful play goes on,
and you may contribute a verse . . .
—*Walt Whitman*

I'LL NEVER FORGET MY FIRST days as a young adult. Just home from my mission and ready for the rest of my life, I packed up my white 1973 Chevy Vega (with sporty black racing stripe) and took off down I-15, headed for college. I knew that Grandpa's sister's used car would turn a lot of heads, and very soon I'd have a day planner full of dates.

It was a new experience to live in my own apartment, pay my own rent, and buy my own groceries. I felt like the little kid in the movie *Home Alone* who, when he discovers that he has the whole house to himself, runs up and down the halls screaming, jumps on the bed, and eats chocolate-drenched ice cream for dinner.

But I hadn't completely lost my head. I still had my anchors. I knew that gospel standards applied even when Mom and Dad weren't around. Some college freshmen don't know how to handle their newfound freedom; they mistake liberty for license. Without the internal control that comes from a testimony, they begin to party and sample some of the forbidden things of the world. But you and I know better. We live the gospel because we *want* to, not because we *have* to. Freedom doesn't mean lack of discipline; freedom *comes* from discipline! So when you leave home, take the anchor of your testimony with you—you'll need it.

Other than your testimony, one of the very most important things you'll need as you head for college or return from a mission is a *purpose.* You need a plan. Now that the track of knowing what you're going to be every other birthday has ended (Beehive/Deacon, Mia Maid/Teacher, etc.), you'll need to chart your own course. It may be school, it may be a mission or marriage, but whatever it is, have a plan. You know the old saying: If you fail to plan, you plan to fail. So make a plan, even if it's only in pencil. It's okay if you need to erase and make alterations. For now, set some goals and plan what you want to do. I love comedian Lily Tomlin's statement: "I always wanted to be somebody. I guess I should have been more specific." Yes, be specific when possible, because if you're headed for nowhere, you'll probably get there.

If You're Through Learning, You're Through

Another word for *graduation* is *commencement,* and that means to start. Your education did not end with the cap and gown; your learning is just beginning. Hopefully you will be able to go to college, even if it's only part-time. Elder Russell M. Nelson once remarked that "the critical difference between your just hoping for good things for mankind and your being able to do good things for mankind is education" ("Reflection and Resolution," *BYU Speeches of the Year, 1989–1990,* p. 65).

Although you've left high school, you're still preparing to make a difference in the world, and part of that preparation is education.

More than in any other time in the world's history, information is available to us at little or no cost. Even if we can't attend college, we can continue to educate ourselves. I read recently that 98 percent of U.S. households have a television set, yet only 2 percent have a library card. We can borrow loads of books at the library, we can listen to books on tape or inspirational tapes while we drive, we can get on the computer and with the touch of a button bring any information we need right before our eyes in a matter of seconds. It's miraculous! I recently purchased a CD-ROM library that gives me access to literally thousands of books for the price of two.

In this church it is obvious that the Lord wants us to keep learning. It will make us better people, better spouses, better fathers and mothers, better missionaries, better employees, and better servants. In the Doctrine and Covenants, the Lord urges us to learn about a variety of things:

> Of things both in heaven and in the earth, and under the earth; things which have been, things which are, things which must shortly come to pass; things which are at home, things which are abroad; the wars and the perplexities of the nations, and the judgments which are on the land; and a knowledge also of countries and of kingdoms—That ye may be prepared in all things when I shall send you again to

magnify the calling whereunto I have called
you, and the mission with which I have com-
missioned you. (D&C 88:79–80)

There's quite a nice list in that verse. I can't think of
any worthwhile topic it doesn't cover. And you'll notice
that the reason for learning is in there too: to be prepared to magnify our callings and serve the world. So,
as you begin your young adult life, make education part
of your plan.

Institutionalize Yourself

Another thing you should be sure to include in your
plan is the institute. Not the kind where nice men in
white coats come to take you away in a straitjacket, but
the kind where the nice men in white shirts take you
down the straight and narrow. The Church has estab-
lished institutes of religion that will help you continue
your gospel study where seminary left off. You don't
have to be a college student to attend (see "Extending
Institute," *Ensign,* October 1997, pp. 39–43). If you're a
young single adult between the ages of eighteen and
thirty, you're in. If you don't know of an institute nearby,
talk to your bishop.

President Gordon B. Hinckley has said:

> Take advantage of every opportunity to
> enlarge your understanding of the gospel.
> Make the effort to participate in seminary and
> institute programs. (*Ensign,* May 1982, p. 42)

> Our great program of Church education
> moves forward. The work of training students
> through the seminary and institute program is

10

constantly being enlarged. . . . We urge all for whom it is available to take advantage of it. We do not hesitate to promise that your knowledge of the gospel will be increased, your faith will be strengthened, and you will develop wonderful associations and friendships. (*Ensign*, May 1984, p. 47)

That's an impressive list of benefits. Not only will your faith and knowledge grow but you will find new friends who believe the things that you do. Outside of your own personal gospel study, your institute classes will be a great place to feel the Spirit, make friends, and keep you anchored to what matters most. There is no knowledge as valuable as gospel knowledge, so make institute part of your plan.

Credit Card Companies Take a Great Interest in You— and from You

Okay, here's a scary one. As soon as it is known by the world that you are a college student, or of college age, credit card companies will want to get you started— or should I say "hooked"—on spending money their way. Be really careful. Unfortunately there are many young adults who can't seem to resist the "buy now, pay later" pitch, and who have gone way into debt. They even use credit to buy fast food.

When you use credit, you are "renting" the money from the credit card company, and the rent you pay is called interest. You've probably heard the old saying about interest: "Thems who understands it, collects it; thems who don't, pays it." That may sound funny, but this topic has a depressing side, too. President J. Reuben Clark described the darker side of interest like this:

> Interest never sleeps nor sickens nor dies; it never goes to the hospital; it works on Sundays and holidays; it never takes a vacation; it never visits nor travels; it takes no pleasure; it is never laid off work nor discharged from employment; it never pays taxes; it buys no food; it wears no clothes; it is unhoused and without home and so has no washing, it has neither wife, children, father, mother, nor kinfolk to watch over and care for; it has no expense of living; it has neither weddings nor births nor deaths; it has no love, no sympathy; it is as hard and soulless as a granite cliff. Once in debt, interest is your companion every minute of the day and night; you cannot shun it or slip away from it; you cannot dismiss it; it yields neither to entreaties, demands, or orders; and whenever you get in its way or cross its course or fail to meet its demands, it crushes you.
>
> So much for the interest we pay. Whoever borrows should understand what interest is; it is with them every minute of the day and night. (Conference Report, April 1938, pp. 102–3)

Credit is not always a bad thing. Most of us will have to go into debt to finance certain long-term expenses like our home or education, but that's where it should stop if possible. Those things are usually referred to as investment debt. What we're talking about is consumer debt.

Try to avoid using a credit card for little things, because little things add up to big things, and that means a big monthly payment. Oddly enough, most people who are deep in credit card debt have a hard time remembering what they bought!

Here's another thing you ought to think of. One of the saddest things that may happen with credit card debt is that you won't get it paid off while you're a student, and you'll bring your debts with you into your marriage. Would you rather marry someone who is $5,000 in debt or someone who has $5,000 in savings? It takes a long time to pay off large credit card debts. The companies plan it that way when they figure the "low monthly minimum payment."

When Elder Jeffrey R. Holland was president of BYU, he and his wife, Patricia, spoke to the young adult student body about a special kind of plastic surgery:

> PAT: . . . Controlling your financial circumstances is another one of those "marriage skills"—and we put that in quotation marks—that obviously matters to everyone and matters *long* before entering into marriage. One of the great laws of heaven and earth is that your expenses need to be less than your income. You can reduce your anxiety and your pain and your early marital discord—indeed, you can reduce your *parents'* anxiety and pain and marital discord right now!—if you will learn to manage a budget.
>
> JEFF: As part of this general financial caution, we encourage, if necessary, plastic surgery for both husband and wife. This is a very

painless operation, and it may give you more self-esteem than a new nose job or a tummy tuck. Just cut up your credit cards. Unless you are prepared to use those cards under the strictest of conditions and restraints, you should not use them at all—at least not at 18 percent or 21 percent or 24 percent interest. No convenience known to modern man has so jeopardized the financial stability of a family— especially young struggling families—as has the ubiquitous credit card. "Don't leave home without it?" That's precisely why he is leaving home—

PAT: and why she is leaving him! (*On Earth As It Is in Heaven* [Salt Lake City: Deseret Book, 1989], pp. 105–6)

It's not a sin to have a credit card. They're handy for emergencies, for travel, and for establishing a good credit rating. But they have to be used carefully.

I once heard some good advice about curbing unnecessary spending that has helped me in my life. In fact, I even made a little card to keep in my wallet that lists three questions to ask before making a purchase: *Do I need it? Do I need it now? Can I live without it?* Also, listening to general conference as a teenager I heard President N. Eldon Tanner give some wonderful financial advice that has stuck with me ever since. His five main points were:

1. Pay an honest tithing
2. Live on less than you earn
3. Distinguish between needs and wants
4. Develop and live within a budget

5. Be honest in all financial affairs (see *Ensign*, November 1979, pp. 81–82)

When the telemarketers call you (and if you are a fresh young adult with no credit history, rest assured that they will), it's really nice to be able to say, "No thanks, I don't have any credit debt, I don't want any credit debt, and I don't need any credit cards. Thank you."

Well, those are just a few important items to be aware of as you begin your new life as a young single adult. The good stuff about dating and courtship is up ahead. We can sum up this chapter in one run-on sentence: Have a plan, keep learning, institutionalize yourself, and don't let the credit card companies take too much interest in you (or from you).

*Results! Why, man, I have gotten
lots of results. I know several thousand
things that won't work.*
—Thomas A. Edison

PARABLE OF THE PIANO

Mawiage. Mawiage is what bwings us togevuh today.
—*The Impressive Clergyman*, The Princess Bride

ONE OF THE FIRST THINGS I realized as a new college student was that there were not enough hours in a day. One afternoon, after feeling a little frustrated with all the demands on my time, I tried to add up all the things I was supposed to be doing. I was in class half the day, and according to the university's recommendations I was supposed to spend two hours studying for each hour spent in class. I had a part-time job (because I had to pay my own tuition) and a time-consuming Church calling. Then, when I'd go to church on Sunday, someone would remind me to spend time each day with the scriptures, keep a journal, and find time for meaningful service. This is how my day looked on paper:

4 hours in class
4 hours working part-time
8 hours studying (2 hours for each class)
7 hours sleeping
1 hour Church calling
1 hour scriptures/journal

25 hours / day

You'll notice that I had to leave out eating, showering, cleaning my apartment, having a life, etc. And even with all that, I've left something else out. You know, the *biggie* (the real reason your mom wanted you to go to college). The one everyone seemed to be interested in when I went home for a visit: "When are you going to get married?" They wanted me to go from a solo to a duet. Somewhere in my 25-hour days I had to find time for a social life. But even when I found the time, I struggled. I never deliberately postponed marriage—I wanted to find someone and get married. I just wasn't very good at it.

An Anonymous Frustration

One Sunday in my student ward, our bishop called for a combined meeting of the Relief Society and priesthood. It was the beginning of the school year, and we were all expecting the usual pre-semester chastity talk. We were not disappointed. The bishop distributed small slips of paper and invited anyone with questions about chastity or dating to write them down, fold them up, and place them in the shoebox that would be making the rounds. After a few audible groans, a handful of people started to write out their questions (aware all the while that those who needed the lesson most weren't even at church).

One of the first questions the bishop read summed up the feelings of many of us in the room: "My problem is not being tempted to break the law of chastity. My problem is getting into a situation where it's actually an option." The room erupted with laughter, and I was delighted because, although I didn't admit it at the time,

I was the one who wrote the question. I wasn't having a problem with the law of chastity; I was having problems just getting a date!

To be honest, I could get dates, but something strange would always happen. Something about looking at my face would cause a girl to tell me what a good "friend" I was, the word *friend* being spoken a little louder than the others. Or my date would pause thoughtfully and say, "You know who you would look good with?" (as if it never occurred to her that I thought *we* might look good together). This was their not-very-subtle method of telling me they weren't interested in me "that way." (Oddly enough, this conversation would usually come up *after* I had paid for dinner. Hmmm.)

What was the deal? Did I have bad table manners? Were there food particles stuck to my face? Perhaps they didn't realize that one day I would grow up, sell the 1973 Vega, and replace it with a sporty red 1978 Ford Fiesta (a real muscle car). Oh well.

Sometimes it was the other way around: I thought of the girl as a "friend," and she was crazy about me. (Seriously! Once or twice someone was crazy about me.) When would I find mutual craziness? I wanted to get married, but things didn't seem to fall into place as easily as they did for so many of my roommates. (Two of my roommates married girls that I had dated first; three other girls I dated decided to go on missions.) I wanted to find a way to explain my frustration, and I finally came up with this little analogy about playing a duet. (Now you understand why I've been using a musical theme in this book.)

Just Duet!

Imagine yourself sitting at the keys of a magnificent grand piano. The lights in the room reflect brightly on the highly polished surface of the ebony-stained wood. You're comfortably situated in a large banquet room filled with people. The music before you is clearly labeled *Matrimony: A Duet.*

Throughout the evening, dinner guests approach the piano with a puzzled look. "Hey," they ask, "why don't you play that music?"

"I'd like to," you respond, "but it's a duet. I need someone to sit here and play it with me."

"Well, you're not trying hard enough," they mutter as they wander off. You wonder to yourself if you could possibly play all the notes the music requires with only ten fingers.

A few moments later someone else notices you sitting all alone and asks, "Hey, how come you're not playing that piece?"

You can't understand why this person hasn't noticed that the music clearly calls for another pianist, but you politely answer, "I'd like to play this song, I really would, but someone has to choose to sit beside me and play it with me. I can't play it alone."

"Oh. Well, you could play it if you had more faith," the person remarks, walking away. *More faith?* You wonder, *Could having more faith give me two more hands?*

You are no longer surprised when a third observer shows up and asks, "Aren't you going to play that piece?"

"I'd really like to," you respond. "I know I should,

and I'm sure the music is beautiful, but someone else, who has agency like I do, has to voluntarily sit beside me and play."

"Well, I think you're just being too picky," comes the advice as the person leaves.

For many of the things we desire in life, we just decide what we want, set our mind to it, work hard, and we can get it. But marriage is different. Someone else is involved, and that changes everything. It's like trying to play a duet with only two hands. In short, *marriage is the only commandment you cannot obey by yourself.* You can obey the law of tithing by yourself, you can keep the Sabbath day holy by yourself, you can observe all of the "thou shalt nots," but you can't keep the commandment to get married by yourself. (Actually, there is another commandment that requires another person—"multiply and replenish the earth"—but it's important to obey the "get married" commandment before you proceed to this one.)

When it comes to matrimony, someone else has to voluntarily join you. Having more faith, trying harder, and being less choosy cannot affect someone else's agency. An all-out war was initiated when Satan sought to destroy the agency of God's children, and the freedom to choose is just as important and inviolate today. You cannot "make" someone fall in love with you, and God will not violate agency.

That's what makes this commandment to get married so interesting. It's different from any other. So don't get too discouraged as you wait for a piano-playing partner. Just remember, when these well-meaning guests approach the piano—as they inevitably will—keep your sense of humor. (The fact is, these people never go away, they just change their questions. As soon as you are married, one of them will approach you and say, "So, when are you going to have a trio?")

What's Your Problem?

Sometimes, those who approach your piano might not understand why you're sitting alone. They only know that you're not married, and that's a problem. But what kind of problem is it? Is it a *value* problem, a *motivation* problem, or a *competency* problem? Let me explain.

Those who are so anxious to see you in a duet might mistakenly assume that you don't *believe* in marriage, or perhaps you just don't understand that it's the right thing to do. That would be a *value* problem.

Perhaps they think you know marriage is right, you just don't *want* to do it. That would be a *motivation* problem.

In my case, I knew I wanted the play the duet, and I believed in the music. My problem? I was incompetent. I didn't know *how* to make it all happen. That's called a *competency* problem (see Stephen R. Covey and Truman G. Madsen, *Marriage & Family: Gospel Insights* [Salt Lake City: Bookcraft, 1983], p. 154). The apostle Paul seemed to be referring to a competency problem when he said, "For to will is present with me; but how to perform that which is good I find not" (Romans 7:18).

I learned the importance of carefully identifying problems when I began speaking regularly to groups of young men. I assumed I should teach them about the "rightness" of serving a mission and fulfilling their priesthood responsibility. For most young men, this is probably appropriate. More than once, however, I have met individual young men who knew they *should* serve a mission (it wasn't a value problem), who *wanted* to serve (it wasn't a motivation problem), but who didn't think they *could*. They were scared to death! They felt incompetent. They were afraid to talk to people, live with a companion, or knock on doors. I was trying to solve a competency problem with a value solution. That's like seeing an eye doctor for a leaky roof.

My guess is that most young single adults, especially the ones who would read this book, don't have a value problem with marriage. They are already convinced that marriage is the right thing to do. They just want to know more about how to make it happen. (If you *do* have a value problem with marriage, this is the wrong book. May I suggest the Doctrine and Covenants, sections 131 and 132.)

This book was not written to try to convince you of the rightness of marriage or the law of chastity. I'm just going to assume you already believe in those things, as I do. We're looking for answers to some of the competency issues—the "how do I do that?" questions.

This Book Is for Bench Sitters

For most young adults out there in Bookland, it's fairly simple: You date, you fall in love, and you get married. But a few of us find that process a little more difficult. Some of us get stuck in the middle, somewhere between dating and falling in love, or between falling in love and getting married. There's potential for a lot of pain in those in-between areas. (As one who struggled myself, I know.) If you find yourself in this category, keep reading. There are some things in here that might help.

The scripture does not say, "Men are that they might have joy, unless they are single," so let's talk about getting joyfully through these in-between years, with plenty of help and advice from Church leaders. Get comfortable there on your piano bench, and we'll start by looking at some "dos" and "don'ts." Then we'll attempt to answer some "whens" and "whos" and "hows." Finally, we'll look at what to do in the meantime, and hopefully we'll end on a good note (so to speak).

Before we get into the Dos and Don'ts

section, I thought we might look

at the evolution of thought

concerning doing and being:

To do is to be—Sartre

To be is to do—Aristotle

To be or not to be—Shakespeare

Do be do be do—Sinatra

De do do do, de da da da—Sting

DON'T FOCUS ON WHAT YOU CAN'T CONTROL

He who worries about calamities suffers
them twice over.
—Og Mandino

A FEW MONTHS AGO, I received a phone call from the nice people at the *New Era* magazine. They asked if I would be willing to submit an article for an upcoming issue devoted to the topic of friendship. I was delighted that they would consider an article of mine for publication. I remember being quite flattered. Then they told me what to write about, and I wondered why they thought I was an expert on the subject. The topic was: "Why Don't I Have Any Friends?"

Anyway, I pondered the question deeply because I had met young people from time to time who had this very problem. Finally, I came up with a half-decent thesis statement: *You can't make people like you, but you can make yourself more likable.* You focus on what you can do, you don't dwell on what you can't do, and you move on. The article suggested that among those things you *can* control are these: you can be clean, you can be curious, and you can be Christlike. (If you'd like to read the whole article, it's in your June 1998 *New Era*.)

I realize I'm writing to young adults this time, but the principle is the same. Many of us, as we begin our new lives as young adults, sour our lives and our moods by focusing on things over which we have no control. We literally give our moods to someone or something else. It's as if we have given control of our happiness away.

For example, I know people who had sleepless nights because their favorite basketball team (okay, it was the Utah Jazz) lost in the NBA finals. I mean, hey, I wanted the Jazz to win too, but I had to keep telling myself, "John, you can't attach how you feel to things you can't control!" (I also wondered if Karl Malone ever paced the floor and lost sleep because he was worried over whether I would do a good job at a fireside. Probably not.) Isn't it interesting that the whole sports world depends on the fact that a bunch of fans will take personally what a group of overpaid, sweaty men do?

As for dating, I used to joke with my other single friends that I usually felt happier, more energetic, and more in love with life when I wasn't dating anyone than when I was. That seemed wrong to me. Wasn't dating supposed to be fun? What was the difference?

Well, when I was dating, I made some mistakes. Sometimes I gave so much importance to what that other person thought of me that I attached all my moods to it. Have you ever done that? If that special someone calls or drops by or gives you a note, you are on cloud nine, you smile, you crank up the loud music as you drive around, and you have a great day. If they don't call, if they don't say hello, if they don't smile at you just the way you expect, you mope and wonder and worry, lose your appetite, turn off the radio, and imagine a multitude of worst-case scenarios about what might have happened.

We focus on what we can't control. This is dangerous, because whenever we use another person's reactions toward us as the sole measuring stick for our own self-worth, we climb aboard a roller coaster with an endless track of ups and downs.

So what do we do? We *try* (and I emphasize the word *try* because all of this is easier said than done) to focus on what we *can* control, and we exercise faith about all the rest.

Looking for Blind Spots

Have you ever tried to change lanes on the highway and been startled by another vehicle's horn? So you quickly swerve into your lane, wondering if you're about to become the latest victim of road rage? Ever done that? Me too. Even with a rearview mirror and fender mirrors, there are certain places you just can't see from the driver's seat. Those are called blind spots. Sometimes we do things in our lives that prevent us from achieving the things we want, and we don't even know it. We may be victims of our personal habits, quirks, or misperceptions. I've heard those types of things called *personal* blind spots.

One time, after being lined up by my roommate for a triple date, I had some of my blind spots revealed to me. The day after our date, the girl I had taken out told my roommate I played the car stereo so loud that when she got home she had a headache. She also felt like I wasn't very interested in her because while the six of us were playing a board game, I started thumbing through a magazine. He also told me that she didn't think I was a very good listener. Me? Not a good listener? I didn't know what to say. Finally I looked at him and said, "Oh, I'm sorry, were you talking to me?"

Joking aside, I was devastated. I never knew I did all that stuff. What kind of a jerk would do that? (Me!) It's a good thing he had the courage to tell me about those things, because I was blind to them. I wouldn't have discovered them on my own. So the next time I was on a date, I muted my 25-watt, 300-amp, 14-inch sub-woofers, put away *Popular Mechanics,* and tried to keep my mouth shut and my eyes and ears open.

I'm grateful to those who love me enough to tell me about my blind spots. It's not a pleasant experience, but once you have your blind spots pointed out, you can do something about changing them. Sometimes it's just a matter of being a little more observant about yourself and others. President Spencer W. Kimball counseled:

> You might take a careful inventory of your habits, your speech, your appearance, your weight, . . . and your eccentricities. . . . Take each item and analyze it. What do you like in others? What personality traits please you in others? Are your dresses too short, too long, too revealing, too old-fashioned? Does your weight drive off possible suitors? Do you laugh

raucously? Are you too selfish? Are you interested only in your own interests or do you project yourself into the lives of others? . . . What
do you do to make yourself desirable? Do you
overdo or underdo? Too much makeup or too
little? Scrupulously clean both physically and
morally? . . . What are your eccentricities, if
any? I think nearly all people have some. If so,
then go to work. Classify them, weigh them,
corral them, and eliminate one at a time. (*The
Teachings of Spencer W. Kimball* [Salt Lake City:
Bookcraft, 1982], p. 295)

We all have good leaders and teachers whom we love
and trust. If you think you might have some blind spots,
you might want to get your courage up and ask one of
them for help. You might say, "If you ever notice that
I'm doing something that's making it harder for me to
succeed, would you tell me about it, please?" Again, it's
easier said than done, and humble pie is sometimes
harder to swallow than a sack of doorknobs, but I'm a
better person today because I did it, and because someone loved me enough to point out some of the things I
couldn't see.

The Not-So-Magnificent Obsession

Whatever you do, don't be obsessed with the fact
that you are single. Some people can't get their minds
off it. They think about it, talk about it, and steer every
conversation in that direction. It doesn't matter what
you say, they'll make a comment about it. For example:
"So, I hear the zoo is expanding." "Yeah, and I'm still
single." Or "Hey, did you know they're closing the

freeway tonight?" "Yeah, and I'm not married." Here's the problem with that: It's not attractive. In fact, it's unattractive. Nobody wants to hang out with someone who can't get their mind off their problems, especially problems they can't control.

On the other hand, there are some people who are always excited. They always have some new adventure or some new project planned. They seem to love life, and they don't obsess over what they can't control. Instead, they tackle what they can control and live life at the top of their lungs. And do you know what? These people are *attractive.* They're fun to be around. Their confidence and enthusiasm for life is contagious. And because of their constant efforts to improve themselves and make a difference in the lives of others, they become better, more interesting, and even more attractive with time. Meanwhile, those who focus on what they can't control just get older.

Lessons from Liberty

Recently my wife and I visited Liberty Jail. What a place! The Church has done a wonderful job of turning what used to be a prison into an inspiring visitors' center. The Prophet Joseph Smith and several others spent the winter of 1838–39 in the basement of this building, sleeping on straw with little protection from the cold. As I looked around the basement cell, surrounded by four-foot-thick stone walls, I asked one of the sister missionaries, "Where is the bathroom?" She explained that the jailers would lower a bucket from an opening in the ceiling. *How horrible,* I thought. No light, no fresh air, no privacy. It's difficult to think of the prophet we all love and respect living in such circumstances. And yet from this place came sections 121, 122, and 123 of the Doctrine and Covenants. In this context, Joseph's words of counsel to the Saints seem even more profound:

> Therefore, dearly beloved brethren, let us cheerfully do all things that lie in our power; and then may we stand still, with the utmost assurance, to see the salvation of God, and for his arm to be revealed. (D&C 123:17)

In other words, do what you can do! Cheerfully! Focus on the things that lie in your power. And go forward with the "utmost assurance" that the Lord is there and aware. If the Prophet can speak of doing things joyfully in such a place, perhaps we can lighten up as well.

Do you want to be happier as a young adult? Do you want to be happier in *life?* Stop worrying about things you can't do anything about, focus on what you can control, work on your blind spots, and give the rest to the Lord. Or, as someone else once put it, "Do your part, do your best, then let go, and let God do the rest."

TAKIN' MY TIME

Well I can't believe what I have just seen,
That beautiful lady was lookin' at me.
She gave me the eye, and I would be wise to give her a try,
But I've been hurt before, I can't take that anymore,
So I'm just . . .

Takin' my time, makin' her mine, no more jumpin' the gun
  from now on,
I'm takin' it slow from the start, got control of my heart,
I'll wait on her 'til I'm sure that she's in love . . .

Well it's goin' well, but it's still hard to tell
Just what the woman is thinkin'
She'll be comin' on strong, but I could do wrong if I begin
  to give in,
And I've been wrong before, I don't want that anymore,
So I'm just . . .

Takin' my time, makin' her mine, no more jumpin' the gun
  from now on,
I'm takin' it slow from the start, got control of my heart,
I'll wait on her 'til I'm sure that she's in love . . .

She's falling in love, she's falling in love, she's falling in
  love, she's falling in love . . .
Well, I've waited enough, I'm sure she's in love,
I think that I'm past the danger,
So I drop by to tell her, and she's with someone else,
And she looks at me like a stranger
Hand in hand they turn to leave, and they walk out the
  door . . .
Now I'm on the floor, was I wrong once more,
Was she just . . .

Takin' my time, leadin' me blind,
Never intending to stay in the end,
Right from the start was she toyin' with my heart,
Havin' some fun 'til she found what she wanted?
Takin' my time, playin' with my mind,
She made me believe that she'd never leave me,
Right from the start she was toyin' with my heart,
Now I'll be payin' the price for weeks to come . . .

DO PLAY THE DATING GAME ACCORDING TO THE RULES

When the One Great Scorer
Comes to write against your name,
He marks—not that you won or lost—
But how you played the game.
—Grantland Rice

ONE OF THE CLASSIC MOVIES of all time, *It's a Wonderful Life,* has a scene in which the young George Bailey is talking with his mother on the front porch. The dialogue goes something like this:

Ma: Can you give me one good reason why you shouldn't call on Mary?

George: Sure, Sam Wainwright.

Ma: Ee-aw?

George: Yeah, Sam's crazy about Mary.

Ma: Well, she's not crazy about him.

George: How do you know? What, did she discuss it with you?

Ma: No . . .

George: Well, then, how do you know?

Ma: Well, I've got eyes, haven't I? Why, she lights up like a firefly whenever you're around. Besides, Sam Wainwright's away in New York and you're in Bedford Falls.

George: And all's fair in love and war?

Ma: Well, I don't know about war . . .

Hmmm. Are there any rules when it comes to the dating game? Or is it a lot like war: Get what you want and destroy the competition? Sounds pretty ruthless.

For you and me, the answer is yes, there are rules. However, it would be impossible to list them all. There are so many possibilities that for every dating dilemma we could pose, the answer would probably be, "It depends." So, rather than try to say there is a hard-and-fast rule for every situation, let's just agree on some guiding principles:

Guiding Principle #1: Honesty

Guiding Principle #2: The Golden Rule

How does that sound? *Honesty* and *the Golden Rule.* That's fairly simple, isn't it? We'll call honesty Guiding Principle 1, or GP1, and the Golden Rule GP2. (This will save a lot of space later on, and it sounds kind of scientific, which adds credibility to this book.)

Another thing we'll need to agree on before we get under way is why we're dating in the first place. When you buy a new board game, you always have to open it up and find the directions. One of the first paragraphs will tell you how to win.

The object of the dating game has changed since you

were a teenager. When you were in high school, you were dating for a different reason. The rules were clearly spelled out in your *For the Strength of Youth* pamphlet: "Go in groups or on double dates . . . later the time will come for choosing just one" (p. 7). Well, now you're out of high school, or home from a mission, and it's *later.* You're dating to build relationships and, hopefully, to find someone to marry. You're discovering what traits you like and which ones you could live without. That's the object of the game. But you have to play the game within the rules.

Asking Someone Out

For guys, one of the most nerve-racking things to do is to ask a girl out (although most of us will never admit it). You want to be smooth, controlled, and totally confident, but sometimes you stumble over your words and sound like a third-grader returning late from recess. Generally speaking, guys haven't learned to communicate as well as girls. While girls spent their teenage years talking and interacting, boys were playing basketball and slugging each other at Scout meetings. Talking to girls is a lot harder than either of those worthwhile activities. There are a few things guys can do, however, to make it a little easier.

In this book, we're going to assume that the boys do most of the asking out. (Your mother will agree.) There are rules about asking for a date that have to do with GP2, our guiding principle of the Golden Rule. Let's look at a bad example first:

Clueless Guy: Are you doing anything tomorrow night?

This one really puts the girl in a bind. Nobody likes

that. You ought to extend to her the luxury of deciding whether she wants to go or not. By asking her if she's "doing anything," you're almost forcing her to consent to go with you, even if the date consists of going to the zoo and cleaning the elephant cages. She has no clue what you want to do, she doesn't know if you're going with friends or alone, and if she says she hasn't got any plans, you've cornered her like a shrewd salesman. Basically, you've broken one of our guiding principles. You wouldn't want to be cornered like that, so don't corner her. That's GP2, the Golden Rule. (A smart way for a girl to answer in that situation would be, "Well, I've got a few things going; what did you have in mind?" Then she can decide if she wants to go with you and Dumbo.) She's a lady. Give her a choice.

Also, you should be asking about a week in advance. Why? Because by asking the night before, you're asking her to reveal whether anyone else asked her out for that weekend. That can be embarrassing, and again, it violates GP2. Most girls, unless they really want to go out with you, will tell you they have plans (even if those plans consist of refilling the salt and pepper shakers) rather than admit on short notice that they don't have a date. And that's their right. Let's consider a better approach:

Clued-in Guy: If you're not doing anything Friday, I was wondering if you'd like to go bowling with me and another couple?

Here's what's good about this method: (1) You're considerate enough not to ask if she has any plans, (2) you're telling her the nature of the date, and

(3) you're telling her that the two of you will be with another couple. Even if she can't go with you, she'll be impressed by the way you asked.

Note: Sometimes guys will take girls to movies that they've already seen or don't want to see. We have to be pretty picky these days. If you're asking someone out to a movie, maybe it's a good idea to sit down together with the newspaper and make a decision both of you can feel comfortable about.

Accepting or Refusing an Invitation

One of the hardest things for a girl to do is hurt a guy's feelings. So sometimes she uses hints instead of direct answers. She uses statements like, "I'm really busy that night," or "I have plans," and hopes that after two or three attempts, the guy will figure it out. Some guys are just plain too dumb to get the hints. Some will ask you out three years in advance just to get you to make a date. Some will keep asking until you say yes. We call this the broken-record tactic: "Well, what about the next week? Well, what about the next week? Well, what about the next week?" Either guys have to learn to hear the real words behind the hints, or girls have to learn to be more direct. Perhaps a little of both would be desirable.

The problem with giving an unclear answer is that the guy might actually believe you. Let's say you don't want to go out, but you say: "Well, I can't, but maybe another time." All you did was tell him to call again. When he does, you'll have the same problem. There may come a time when a girl has to be *completely* honest. Some girls are able to do this on the first call; others find it much too hard. How do you tell a guy you don't want to go out with him without violating GP2? Answer: You tell him the truth (GP1) as kindly as possible (GP2). Cherie Gray, author of *The Dating Book* (© 1996), recommends this response: "Thank you. I appreciate your asking, but I really can't," or "Oh, I'm sorry, but I'm not interested in going out. Thank you for asking, though" (p. 63). These responses are clear, direct, and unambiguous—in other words, honest (GP1). Speaking as a guy, I would much rather get that response on my first phone call than spend time, money, and energy waiting for the real truth. However, I do understand how that kind of direct honesty can be very difficult. If you sense that a guy is too dumb to understand a hint, try to be honest and direct without being mean. That's the way you'd want to be turned down, right? Remember GP2: Decline dates with others as you would have others decline dates with you.

If you're a guy, you might as well get started on learning the skill of listening between the lines. You'll need it even when you're married. If a girl really has a legitimate excuse, and she wants you to call again, listen for something like, "Please call me again," or "I hope you'll ask another time." If she doesn't say something like that, or if she's talking to you as if you were selling aluminum siding, well, perhaps you should take the hint.

Girls have their own rules about this issue. Some girls feel that any guy who has the nerve to ask deserves one date. Others feel that if they already know they don't like this guy, why waste time for both of them and get his hopes up? Sorry, no guarantees. All you can do is use your guiding principles and do the best you can.

Return Appointments and "The Talk"

Let's say you go on the bowling date, and you have a great time. (In this example, we'll say you're a girl.) At the doorstep, you drop a hint like, "I had a really fun time," which, being interpreted, is, "Call me again." So you go out a few more times, and your feelings begin to grow. Questions come up in your head: "Does he like me as much as I like him?" "I wonder how he feels about me." "Is he dating other girls?" You want to ask him about it, but you hesitate. You want to have "the talk." In dating circles, we often call it the "Where Do We Stand" or "D.T.R." (Define the Relationship) talk. You want to know where this thing is going.

Having this little talk is necessary, but forcing it too soon can be dangerous. To paraphrase Neal A. Maxwell, "You don't rip up the plant to see how the roots are doing." Of course, you should be honest (GP1), but being honest doesn't mean wearing your heart on your sleeve. Jesus was honest, but he didn't cast his pearls before swine. (Oops, that would make the person you're dating a swine, so let's change it to casting your pearls "before their time.") A proverb says, "A fool uttereth all his mind: but a wise man keepeth it in until afterwards" (Proverbs 29:11). Also, there is "a time to keep silence, and a time to speak" (Ecclesiastes 3:7).

The thing about having this talk is that once you've had it, it will completely change the atmosphere of your dating relationship. This "where do we stand" talk marks the invisible boundary between "dating for fun" and "dating seriously." It may reveal that one of you is taking things much more seriously than the other. If your friend is still in the "having fun/getting to know you" stage, it may scare him or her off when the possibility of future dates would otherwise remain.

Also, even after you've had this talk the first time, rest assured, you'll have to have it again. So take your time. If possible, be patient. Relax; get to know one another. There will come a time when you should talk, but let it happen naturally. The goal is to have it occur at a time when *both* of you want to talk. This way, you can both be in the driver's seat.

Elder Boyd K. Packer observed:

> There is a phenomenon involved in courtship that is as strange as anything in human behavior. When a boy and a girl start to relate to one another, if the boy feels a heavy attraction for a girl and pursues her too strongly, surely he will be repulsed. And if a girl is too forward with a boy to whom she is attracted, he will reject her immediately. About all she has to do is telephone him twice and that ends that. While it is absolutely necessary that this deep attraction take place, if one or the other of the partners makes an expression of it too soon, the relationship is destroyed. In the early stages of courtship, if that happens, we say something like this: "I can't stand anybody who really wants me." It reminds me of Groucho Marx, who received an invitation to join a prominent San Francisco club. He sent the invitation back with the notation, "Any club that would have people like me in it isn't fit to join."

This strange phenomenon of human behavior I think maybe has a purpose, and I have wondered if the Lord did not structure it that way, to prevent us from getting together prematurely or too easily, too early. Fortunately there comes a time when they both feel the attraction in about the same intensity and love has blossomed. (*Eternal Love* [Salt Lake City: Deseret Book, 1973], pp. 9–10)

One thing you'll notice is that whoever has the lower level of commitment is in control of the relationship. If you are too impatient and try to force a decision, it could spoil things. So take your time. This is another guiding principle you might want to add to your list: patience.

Steady As She Goes

Perhaps after "the talk," you've both decided that you don't want to date anyone else. We call this "going steady" or dating exclusively. I suppose the purpose of this arrangement is to allow you to spend more time together, get to know one another better, and see if you are compatible in all the ways that are important to you.

It's also a time when you may be more willing to show affection in public, such as holding hands. Be aware that this sends a message to everyone around you. A girl might as well wear a blinking neon sign around her neck that says, "Don't ask me out, I have a boyfriend."

The sharing of affection brings up more unwritten rules of the dating game. For example, it's almost assumed that if you are holding hands or kissing someone, you are going steady with that person. On the other hand, if you're dating two different people and kissing them both, you're breaking the rules, don't you think? In fact, if you're dating two different people and holding hands, it ought to cause some discomfort in the governing-principles part of your brain.

The only other thing I'd say about going steady is to be especially careful to bridle your passions during this time. Going steady doesn't excuse anything, and the law of chastity doesn't change just because you're dating exclusively. In fact, this is a time to be more careful than ever before. The marriage decision involves your head and your heart. Even when your behavior is well within the boundaries of the law of chastity, expressing affections too freely can make it harder for you to think rationally about your relationship. (We've devoted a whole chapter to expressing affection later on.)

Being "Too Nice"

With all this talk of honesty and "do unto others," some of the guys out there may respond, "Girls are turned off by a guy who is too nice." You're right, some are. But that's okay. The memory of you will haunt them when their husband nightly parks his body in front of ESPN and demands his dinner. Besides, being nice doesn't mean being a doormat, or being insecure. It just means that you govern yourself by true principles, like GP2. The girls you date might not appreciate it, but believe me, the woman you marry will love it.

I suppose it is possible to try to be so accommodating that you sound terribly insecure. Here's an extreme example:

"Oh, did I come too early? Oh, I'm sorry. I mean, I could go sit in the car for a while. I always do things like this. Anyway, I'm really sorry. Okay, well, let's go to the car. Hey, it's not really a great car, I mean, it's kind of old, but I cleaned it today. I hope you don't mind riding in it. Okay, um, are you comfortable? I could move the seat up if you want. Is it too cold in here? Okay, I'll turn up the heater, and you just tell me, okay? Is everything okay? You probably feel dumb being seen with me, huh?"

Going out with someone like this would be exhausting. By all means, be nice, but have a healthy dose of self-assurance as well. That's a wonderfully attractive combination. Maybe there's a better way to say all of the same things without sounding like a worrywart. How about:

"Hey, am I early? Wow, you guys have a cool apartment. Hi, I'm Ted. Are you Julie's roommate? Where are you from? Oh, I love it up there. So how's school? [What a nice guy! He introduces himself to all the roommates.] Hi, Julie, you ready? Hey, it was nice meeting you guys, see you later. Julie and I are flying to Bermuda for dinner on the beach, so we'll see you all later. [As you walk to the car:] I got the '73 Vega tonight; my roommates were fighting me for it. Listen, you're climate-control specialist for the evening, so you adjust that however you want, okay?"

The old saying is that "nice guys finish last." Don't believe it. Nice guys win before they even start. I know that there are some girls out there who are terribly attracted to guys who treat them like dirt. This is a phenomenon that has baffled men for centuries.

Perhaps it's the guy version of "playing hard to get." It involves the human tendency to desire most the things you cannot have. Perhaps this is what Longfellow was talking about when he said, "The men that women marry, and why they marry them, will always be a marvel and a mystery to the world." I don't have the answer. Maybe when you figure it out you can write a book on it. Call it *What John Left Out of What He Wished He'd Known When He Was Single.* Whatever the reason for this strange behavior by both sexes (guys also sometimes go after girls who treat them badly), it's no excuse for not being nice. When guiding principles are true principles, live by them and you can't lose.

When You and Your Roommate Like the Same Person

What do you do when you and your roommate end up wanting to date the same person? This is a scary one, but again, guiding principles should govern your actions. Be kind, don't burn any bridges, and recognize that if you do things right, you need not have any regrets later on.

I was completely smitten over a girl once, and I spent a considerable amount of time and energy trying to make things happen. She decided one day that we were just friends, and she wanted to serve a mission. I went through the usual breakup woes and went on with life, but my feelings for her remained. While she was gone, I found out that both my roommate and I had been writing to her. Shortly after her return eighteen months later, I found out that she and my roommate had been going out. One weekend, dateless, I was sitting on the couch watching the adventures of Captain Picard when my roommate and this girl who had dumped me came walking into the apartment. They were laughing hysterically about how his car had just broken down. The only thing I could think of was how I wanted to beam up. Then my roommate asked me if I could drive them both to her house so he could drop her off. Oh, if I'd only had a phaser. Embarrassed beyond belief, I held my peace and drove them to her home while they talked and laughed in the backseat. I wanted to lean back and say, "Don't worry, I know the way." When we arrived, I watched as they walked to the doorstep; then I looked at the floor mats to make the tension go somewhere else. I was amazed that my roommate didn't know this was killing me, but I didn't say a thing.

Believe it or not, about a week later it happened again. "Hi, could you give me and the girl who dogged you a ride home?" I drove them home again, feeling doubly embarrassed the whole time. From then on, whenever I knew those two were going out, I went out too, whether I had a date or not. I'd find other ways to do service projects for my roommate, thank you.

Anyway, a while later, they broke up. And, much to my surprise, I had the chance to take her out again. We dated and both discovered that we should probably remain just friends. Had I blown up the first time, I probably wouldn't have been able to date her again and settle the situation in my own heart. I still see both of these people from time to time, and I'm so glad I have nothing to regret. I didn't speak any harsh words, pass any judgments (at least not out loud), or burn any bridges, and I'm grateful.

So what do you do if your roommate likes the same

person you do? You behave so that if you have the chance to date the person later, you can do so with no regrets. I know a girl whose roommate tried to destroy her reputation because they liked the same person. I don't know about you, but I would not want to be called to account for that kind of juvenile behavior. There's nothing attractive about being vindictive and jealous. If you're in a similar situation, be your real self throughout, governed by your principles and not your passions. The person your roommate is dating will probably notice.

Another thing that helps in these situations is to simply keep the faith. Keep the faith! You never know how things will work out, and you might as well remain hopeful and happy. It's times like these that give us the opportunity to see if we really trust in the Lord as we have been taught, or if we'd prefer to worry and stew and hurt.

Closing Thoughts

The dating game has many rules. Unfortunately, no one knows what they are. I mean, many of them haven't been written down. But you don't need them in writing; you have the gospel, and you know that Jesus taught us to love one another as he loved us. There isn't a lot about dating in the scriptures, so just remember, when in doubt, go back to guiding principles.

Is all fair in love and war? Probably not. Use good judgment, and remember that the object of the dating game is to make it to the temple with no regrets. On that day, one of your greatest satisfactions can come from the knowledge that you followed true principles and played by the rules.

Here's one of those funny paragraphs that get passed around the office. I thought it was perfect for a book for singles:

We have not succeeded in answering your problem. The answers we have found only seem to raise more questions. In some ways we feel we are as confused as ever. But we feel that we are confused on a higher level, and about more important things.

DON'T CONTINUE TO DATE SOMEONE YOU KNOW YOU WOULDN'T MARRY

If this ain't love, you gotta let me go.
—Huey Lewis

IT SEEMS INCREDIBLY OBVIOUS, doesn't it, that you shouldn't go on dating someone you know you wouldn't marry? You'd think so, but believe it or not, many young adults struggle with this one.

Elder Bruce C. Hafen gave a wonderful talk, "The Gospel and Romantic Love," to a young adult audience when he was president of Ricks College. I liked one sentence in that talk so much that I made it the title of this chapter:

> Don't date someone you already know you would not ever want to marry. If you fall in love with someone you should not marry, you can't expect the Lord to guide you away from that person after you are already emotionally committed. (*Ensign,* October 1982, p. 67)

Why shouldn't you date someone you know you couldn't marry? Well, for one thing, it's a waste of time for both of you (because it takes you away from more promising relationships). Second, you could hurt someone's feelings. But there's a third thing in there that's very important. Let's look at that quote again: "If you fall in love with someone you should not marry . . ." Whoa, did you catch that? You mean it's possible to fall in love with someone that you *shouldn't* marry? Absolutely. So you'd better be careful who you date, 'cause you marry who you date!

"Falling in love" is a difficult experience to define. Most of what we believe about falling in love comes from TV shows, songs on the radio, or movies we've seen. Gee, there's a fine source of information for how to govern your life. If when you meet someone you suddenly hear music in the background, then you know you're falling in love! And here's another frightening fallacy from Hollywood: The feeling of "falling in love" is a sign! It's fate! It's Cupid! It's the cosmos telling you you've met "the right person"! (This is especially true if there are good special effects.)

Not so, says Elder Hafen. You can fall in love with someone you shouldn't marry.

What do the scriptures have to say about falling in love? Well, I thought I'd see what I could find one day, and of course I turned to one of my heroes, Nephi. Surely we could learn from his experiences with dating, courtship, and marriage, couldn't we? In 1 Nephi 16:7 we see that Nephi accomplished in only one sentence what this entire book is trying to cover: "And it came to

56

pass that I, Nephi, took one of the daughters of Ishmael to wife." Wow. Mr. "go and do" just "went and did," and that was the end of it. We have very little detail on how it all happened for Nephi.

The fact is, there isn't a lot in the scriptures about what our modern culture calls "falling in love." But we do learn quite a bit about the guiding principle of honesty. We do learn about integrity. We learn that we ought to treat our neighbors the way we want to be treated. So here's the point: *It's dishonest to date someone you know you would not ever want to marry.* It's also not very nice. If you have the idea that you can just keep dating this person until you find what you *really* want in someone else, isn't that a little unkind? Even if you do get free dinners?

Of course, this isn't to say that you shouldn't give someone a fair chance. It may take a few dates to find out if the relationship has potential or not. The point is, *if you're sure* it's not going anywhere, the kindest thing to do is break it off.

Sometimes we know we should break off a relationship, but we're too scared. We might even say to ourselves, "But I don't want to hurt this person." Well, folks, here's one of the hard realities of dating and courting. Sometimes, in a dead-end relationship, you might think the choice is between hurting someone and not hurting someone. Wrong. It may be that the only choice you're left with is whether to hurt someone *a little* or *a lot.* And the longer you prolong a relationship that isn't going to work, the greater the hurt will be.

Brother Gawain Wells, a psychologist, explains:

It feels good to invest in a relationship. To care. To want to share. To want to give.

If your dating relationship feels joyous and healthy, if both of you feel the Lord's approval of your decision to marry, then the relationship "works," and you marry. If it doesn't work, you don't marry. There is no third alternative.

However, many people assume there *is* a third alternative and try to keep the relationship alive when all signs of vitality have ceased. Both in my church callings and in my profession as a clinical psychologist, I have worked with people who cannot accept breaking up as a healthy part of the selection process of courtship. Instead, they see it as a time to punish themselves, to feel hurt, or even to try and hurt others.

. . . Sometimes it's better for two people not to marry each other. They would both be happier married to other people. It's that simple. Perhaps they've formed a relationship for the wrong reasons. But even when the motives are right, a relationship still might not have that "spark" that impels *both* toward marriage. In such cases, breaking up is often the kindest alternative. ("Breaking Up without Going to Pieces," *Ensign*, June 1982, pp. 58–61)

Well, We're Just Dating for Fun

After hearing all of this, some may ask, "What about just dating for fun?" Good point. (If you're a young man preparing for a mission, this is probably the kind of dating that you're doing—just building wholesome friendships but avoiding forming serious ones. See *For the Strength of Youth*, p. 7.)

Some young people say they are just dating for fun, and yet they're kissing. Does that seem right to you? I hope not. There's a mixed message in there. Most of us have a lot of friends—do we kiss all of our friends? Probably not. Also, if you're really just dating for fun, you are probably spending time with many different people. Are you kissing all the people you're dating "just for fun"? If so, there's a problem. Kissing is *serious* business involving people's feelings. It's not for recreation. (We'll dedicate a whole chapter to this topic later on.)

In short, if you really believe you're dating as "just friends," then be sure to act like it. How could we best define "dating for fun"? Well, personally, I wouldn't even use the word *dating*. Perhaps we could say we're just building or continuing friendships, without sharing affection, and both of us know it.

Often, one person might think, "Well, we're just friends, and we just go out and have fun," but the other person may be secretly hoping for something else to develop. If you feel like "something else" isn't going to happen, he or she needs to know. There has to be some kind of understanding between the two of you.

In any case, the things we're talking about here are serious. When you spend a lot of time with someone, you're building something. You're building a relationship. And it's possible to develop attachments to someone you shouldn't marry. And then you have to "break up" the attachment. And that's why we've spent a whole chapter on this one sentence. To avoid heartache and breakups for yourself and others, take Elder Hafen's advice: *Don't date someone you already know you would not marry.*

BOYS

A heart is not a plaything, a heart is not a toy,
But if you want it broken, just give it to a boy.
Boys, they like to play with things to see what
    makes them run,
But when it comes to kissing, they do it just for fun.
Boys never give their hearts away; they play us
    girls for fools,
They wait until we give our hearts and then
    they play it cool.
You'll wonder where he is at night; you'll wonder
    if he's true.
One moment you'll be happy; one moment you'll be blue.
If you get a chance to see him, your heart begins to dance.
Your life revolves around him—there's nothing
    like romance.
And then it starts to happen: you worry day and night.
You see, my friend, you're losing him, it never
    turns out right.
Boys are great, though immature; the price you pay is high.
He may seem sweet and gorgeous, but remember, he's a guy.
Don't fall in love with just a boy; that takes a lot of nerve.
You see, my friend, you need a man to get what you deserve.
So when you think that you're in love, be careful if you can,
Before you give your heart away, make sure that he's a man.

—Author unknown

DO EXPRESS AFFECTION CAREFULLY

Georgie Porgie, pudding and pie,
Kissed the girls and made them cry . . .

They draw near to me with their lips,
but their hearts are far from me . . .

WHAT DO YOU DO WHEN you get home from a date? Well, it depends.

If you're a girl:

If it was a bad date, you go straight to the fridge, gather all your roommates around (or your mom and sisters), and tell them *every single detail* over bowls of ice cream.

If it was a good date, you go straight to the fridge, gather all your roommates around (or your mom and sisters), and tell them *every single detail* over bowls of ice cream.

If you're a boy:

If it was a bad date, you walk in the house, eat a bowl of Cap'n Crunch, and go to bed.

If it was a good date, you walk in the house, eat a bowl of Cap'n Crunch, and go to bed.

Okay, I'm generalizing a little bit. Most of us, especially if it was a good date, will rewind the tape and watch it over again in our minds. We'll try to remember each word that was spoken and ask ourselves, "What did that mean?" More important than the words, however, are the actions. Actions speak louder than words, right? If I'm on a date and I crack a joke, and my date grabs my elbow and gives it a little squeeze, she hasn't used any words, but WOW has she communicated! If that happened to me, I would say to myself, "Hmmm. I think she's interested in me."

This is why we have to be careful. If I put my arm around someone, I'm not using any words, but my actions say, "I like you." If I hold someone's hand, the message is a little stronger, "I really like you." If I kiss my date, the message is loud and clear, and it's right up there with "I love you."

Would you say "I love you" to someone if you really didn't feel that strongly? Of course not. That would be lying. Would you kiss someone, in effect saying "I love you," when in reality you were only mildly interested? It's possible to lie with our actions just as it is to lie with our words.

Elder Marvin J. Ashton said: "A lie is *any* communication given to another with the intent to deceive. . . . A lie can be effectively communicated without words ever being spoken" (*Ensign*, May 1982, p. 9).

In our age of modern media and eroding values, expressions of affection have lost much of their meaning.

President Spencer W. Kimball taught, "Kissing has been prostituted and has degenerated to develop and express lust instead of affection, honor, and admiration. To kiss in casual dating is asking for trouble. *What do kisses mean* when given out like pretzels, and robbed of sacredness?" (*The Teachings of Spencer W. Kimball,* Edward L. Kimball, ed. [Salt Lake City: Bookcraft, 1982], p. 281; emphasis added).

A Kiss Is a Commitment

Some young adults may view expressions of affection as "just for fun." They may think that kissing is okay as recreation. But those actions are powerful and sacred, and they communicate a high level of commitment. This is why we must be careful. Elder Bruce C. Hafen counseled:

> Always be emotionally honest in the expression of affection. Sometimes you are not as careful as you might be about when, how, and to whom you express your feelings of affection. . . . When any of you—men or women—are given entrance to the heart of a trusting young friend, you stand on holy ground. In such a place, you must be honest with yourself—and with your friend—about love and the expression of its symbols. ("The Gospel and Romantic Love," *Ensign,* October 1982, p. 67)

Some young men may get caught up in the "conquest" mentality when it comes to affection. It's not hard to see where they could have learned this. If you've ever seen a group of guys on a sitcom, you've probably noticed that when one of them comes home from a date, they all want to know if he "scored." Unfortunately, much of modern media has turned dating into a contest and kissing into points on a scorecard. Brother Randal A. Wright wrote about a young man in his seminary class who bragged that he had kissed six girls in one day. Brother Wright was looking forward to talking to him:

> I asked about his ideas on kissing. He let me know that he thought he should kiss as many girls as possible before his mission, to see if he was compatible with any. I asked him how many girls he had kissed. His response: "So many that I can't keep count! In fact, I really don't believe if they all walked through the door right now I would even recognize them all." I was surprised, but smiled so he'd keep talking. I finally asked, "How many in one day?" "Six," came the quick reply. "And that was all before 2:00 P.M. I stayed with the same girl after that for the rest of the day." He told me that he was at a high school event when this took place. I asked if the girls were LDS. He slowly shook his head, but quickly added that it wasn't a date. . . . The next day, when I saw the young man again, I said: "Guess what! Your kissing record has been beaten!"
>
> "No way! I know no one around here has beaten it," came his startled reply.
>
> "Yes, it happened!"
>
> "Who?"

"Your future wife!" I calmly replied. "She had the same goal as you, and kissed seven different nonmember guys in one day." (*Feeling Great, Doing Right, Hanging Tough* [Salt Lake City: Bookcraft, 1991], p. 105)

This was the first time the young man saw the shoe on the other foot. My question is, did each of those young women realize that she was only a notch on the way to his goal? Or did they think, "Wow, he really likes me! He cares about me." These expressions of affection are closely connected to our feelings, and it is unkind and insensitive to treat them so lightly. President Thomas S. Monson warned, "Men, take care not to make women weep, for God counts their tears" (*Ensign*, November 1990, p. 47).

Any young adult who is paying attention has heard many talks on the law of chastity. We've heard about it in seminary, we've read about it in *For the Strength of Youth,* and we've even heard apostles and prophets speak powerfully on the subject in general conference. One indicator of the spirituality of the people you date is their respect for the law of chastity and their conduct concerning expressions of affection. Their attitude before marriage gives you an idea of what their attitude will be after marriage. Elder Hugh Pinnock taught, "Men and women who do not have a wholesome respect for regulations during the dating process will often continue to break the rules after the word 'yes' at the altar is spoken" ("Ten Keys to Successful Dating and Marriage Relationships," *BYU Fireside and Devotional Speeches, 1981,* p. 70).

We have been asked by our leaders to be careful with expressions of affection not because they are bad, but because they are good. In fact, the only word that seems to describe them properly is *sacred.*

When a relationship becomes too physical, it becomes harder to tell whether you care about the person because of who he or she is, or just because you've developed emotional attachments by expressing affection. One good way to tell if things have become too physical is to agree not to touch each other for a week or two. See if you really enjoy each other's company, or if you are using physical intimacy to make up for a lack of emotional intimacy. Brother Gawain Wells has written: "A couple's physical attraction to one another may mask an inability to communicate. Some couples may know how to kiss but don't know how to talk to each other. For them, the physical aspect of their relationship is something they fall back on to avoid developing caring and communication" ("Breaking Up without Going to Pieces," *Ensign,* June 1982, pp. 58–61).

It feels wonderful to feel close to someone physically. But these feelings are very powerful and can lead to much pain if not handled carefully. It is better for many reasons to be very conservative when it comes to physical affection. First, the Lord has asked us many times and in many ways to bridle our passions (see Alma 38:12). Second, when you hold off on too much affection, you are able to think more clearly about the relationship and make better decisions concerning its future. Third, if you do break up, the pain and embarrassment will be a lot less than if you shared a lot of affection. Also, the chances are very good that you will see this person again, maybe even in future Church assignments. At those times, you don't want to have to feel embarrassment and regret in his or her presence.

The danger in writing all these cautions about affection is that someone might misunderstand and say, "Kissing is bad." Wrong, hold it, stop the presses. That's not it at all. Kissing is not bad. However, kissing and other expressions of affection send powerful messages that others believe and act on. Just make sure your actions match your words; otherwise, they're dishonest and harmful. Two thousand years ago, someone's actions didn't match his words. Listen to the stinging rebuke: "Judas, betrayest thou the Son of man with a kiss?" (Luke 22:48). Judas used a symbol of affection as a tool of betrayal. Our actions should not betray our true intentions either.

So what do you do when you get home from a date? Well, after the Cap'n Crunch and the ice cream, you sleep peacefully because you were honest and true to yourself and your date. Then you can wake up the next morning and see your own reflection with a clear conscience. Elder Russell M. Nelson taught, "The first morning's glance in the mirror cannot reflect joy if there is any recollection of misdeeds the night before. The surest step toward joy in the morning is virtue in the evening. Virtue includes courtesy to companions all day long" (*The Power within Us* [Salt Lake City: Deseret Book, 1988], p. 77).

WHY IS A DAY PLANNER BETTER THAN A GIRLFRIEND?

1. A day planner will never make you late.
2. You don't have to pay attention to your day planner if you don't want to.
3. Your day planner will still be there when you get off your mission.
4. If you lose your day planner, it won't keep your tapes and sweaters.
5. You only have to pay for your day planner once.
6. You never have to worry about someone else using your day planner.
7. Your day planner will wait for you in the car while you play basketball.
8. A day planner doesn't care if you have another planner.
9. Your day planner already comes with rings.

WHY DAY PLANNERS ARE BETTER THAN BOYFRIENDS

1. Day planners don't have their own agenda.
2. Day planners are organized.
3. Day planners don't need to be fed.
4. Day planners are concerned with your schedule.
5. Day planners don't forget your birthday, anniversary, or other important dates.
6. Day planners don't mind being claimed in public.
7. Day planners aren't sealed books.
8. Day planners contain meaningful information.
9. When you schedule a date with a day planner, it doesn't expect anything in return.

—Author unknown

DON'T LET BREAKUPS BREAK YOU UP

Breaking up is hard to do.
—Neil Sedaka

She's breaking up! She's breaking up!
—Scotty

SOMETIMES, WITHIN THE FIRST three or four seconds of a first date, you know that the two of you would never work. Sometimes it takes the whole evening or maybe even a few dates to figure this out. At other times, you meet someone and begin to date, and everything feels great. You wonder if this could be *the one.* Although you hardly know each other, you imagine your new friend to be perfect in every way. You fill in all the gaps with the best things you can imagine. To you, the person already has all the traits, talents, and skills that you hope he or she possesses.

With time, however, you may discover that some of the things you *thought* were there are not. Reality is a little different. After a while you may begin to ask,

SEVENTH MOVEMENT: IMPROVISATION

"Could I really marry this person? Did I make him or her into something that wasn't real?" Slowly but surely, you're coming down to earth. It's okay. It happens to all of us. And, more than likely, the same thing may be going on in the other person's mind. Usually this will lead to the sometimes painful experience we call a breakup. It's tough. But after a while, you'll get your courage back and start all over again.

Most of us will go through this kind of cycle many times before we get married. Gee, there's a happy thought. That's why people say they get tired of "the dating game." It's expensive—emotionally as well as financially.

For many of us, the dating cycle is like a broken washing machine. It goes through the presoak, the wash, the soak, maybe a little break to add fabric softener, but somehow never gets to the rinse and spin. Oh well. It's all part of the process, and sometimes it's not very much fun. (What do you do with an armful of soapy clothes?)

How do you know when you ought to break up? Here are a few danger signs that may indicate that a relationship is in trouble.

1. You begin to feel obligated. Things you should freely want to do for the other person become tasks you do only because you are expected to do them. You're dating *seriously.* (When people used to ask me if I was dating anyone serious, I would always say, "No, the girls I date are pretty lighthearted.")

2. You begin to test each other. "If he loves me, he'll do what I want." "If she really likes me, she'll be glad to go with me, even if I'm calling half an hour before the party." You try to find out, "Do you enjoy being with me as much as I enjoy being with you?"

3. You feel you can't communicate on the same level. The things that are exciting or interesting to you aren't interesting to your partner. You don't feel "fulfilled" when you talk or share experiences. Some couples, when they get to this point, substitute physical affection for their lack of emotional intimacy.

4. You feel lonely and think about other people. You find yourself daydreaming about other things you could be doing or other people you could go out with. Even when the two of you are together, you feel lonely.

5. You feel like a low priority. The other person's level of commitment to the relationship differs from yours. You feel as if you are an interruption to the other person, as if you're not important. (I knew a lot of girls who were always trying to decide, "Should I go on a mission or study abroad in Jerusalem?" Men occupied a lower spot on their list of priorities.)

Another Interrupted Wash Cycle for Me

(In keeping with our musical theme, please recall the theme song to *The Brady Bunch* as you read the next bit.)

> *Here's a story*
> *'Bout a man named Johnny,*
> *Who was busy as a student at the "Y."*
> *He's an RM, with a good future,*
> *But still a single guy.*

Okay, that's enough of that.

Let me tell you about a time when I got "dumped." I had taken this girl out to dinner a few times and on a few other casual dates, and I thought something good might develop. But on the way home from our seventh or eighth date, she became really serious and asked if she could talk to me inside for a minute. "Uh oh," I thought, "here it comes." We entered her apartment and sat on the couch, and I listened as she struggled to put her thoughts into words. I could tell it was hard for her. She looked uncomfortable, and although she was telling me she didn't like me "that way," I was appreciative. I respected her for being willing to be honest, to tell me face to face that she wanted to be "just friends." We talked for another minute or two, smiled and laughed a little, and then I left. (Back to the *Brady Bunch* theme song:)

> *The breakup lunch,*
> *I had a hunch,*
> *That's the way I survived the breakup lunch.*

Was it fun? Not at all. In fact, it hurt a little bit. There I was, interrupted once again midcycle with an armful of soapy laundry. *However,* I would much rather have it happen that way than by one of the other common but less direct methods: having her roommates repeatedly tell me she wasn't home, or having her tell me she was busy each time I called, or having her tell me who I would look good with, or some other honesty-avoiding, hint-dropping, pain-prolonging strategy. Yes, folks, honesty is still the best policy.

Making It through a Tough Breakup

How do you handle a breakup without letting it break you up? Well, it's never easy. And if you've been dating someone for a long time, it can be excruciating.

But you and I have a blessing of inestimable worth. We have the gospel. We have perspective. I have had some tough breakups, and the very best thing to help me through was my understanding of the plan of salvation. B. H. Roberts once said, "Faith is trust in what the spirit learned eons ago." Deep down in my spirit, I knew that someday I would be married and have a family. I trusted what my spirit knew. That was the spark of hope I needed to carry on.

If you've been on the receiving end of a breakup—or, in other words, if someone you were dating started using the word *friend* a lot—here are a few suggestions that might help.

Take your time. Some breakups can really hurt, and I mean big-time hurt, like getting-hit-by-a-dump-truck hurt. You can't expect to get over something like that overnight. Ecclesiastes tells us that there is a time to mourn, and sometimes you're just going to feel sad for a while. It's important to work through these feelings. Take things one day at a time. If you don't know how you're going to make it through an entire day, take it an hour at a time, or a minute at a time. Beware of the tendency to endlessly "replay the tape" and relive your mistakes and failures over and over. It may be that you have to celebrate small daily triumphs to realize that you're making progress. For example, "I only cried three times today!" Eventually, the time will come when you truly desire to heal and move on.

Once again, it is not easy. There's no tricky way over or around the hurt. Sometimes the only way through is through. But what you're feeling is not unique to you.

It's what a good portion of the songs on the radio are about. Other people have eventually made it through things like this, and you will too.

Write! It's very therapeutic to put things in black and white. Try writing your experience all out in your journal. Sometimes the situation will become clearer to you when you get it out of your head and onto paper. Who knows, you may write a bestseller or a classic breakup song like "Feelings."

Change the scenery. In order to put a broken relationship behind you, it might help to rearrange the furniture, buy some new clothes, or get some new music that has no connection with the past. Start a new hobby or a new book. Do something you've never done before. Make yourself some new memories so you'll have something else to think about and remember. Be outside in fresh air and sunshine. Go running or biking and get your blood flowing.

Be with people. You may want to spend a lot of time by yourself at first while you sort things out. But the time will come when you will be anxious to put the past behind you. When you're ready, spend time with people; go to parties or to movies. You'll discover that for a few brief moments each day, you won't think of the breakup. Eventually those brief moments will grow into periods of several minutes, or maybe even an hour. This is more evidence that you're healing.

Watch your mouth. As soon as your friends find out you broke up, everyone will want to know, "Did you break it off with him/her, or did he/she break it off with you?" Keep it to yourself if you want. Just be careful what you say. Brother Gawain Wells has written:

> If you've been hurt in a relationship, you may think it's understandable that you defend yourself by denigrating or criticizing the other person. Actually, it's a way of running away from reality, and it's a childish and defensive gesture. Whatever has not worked out, the Lord requires that we forgive all people—and this commandment is as true in a dating relationship as in any other. Bitterness is never the right solution. ("Breaking Up without Going to Pieces," *Ensign*, June 1982, pp. 58–61)

Stay close to the Lord. Keep saying your prayers and bringing the Spirit into your life by reading the scriptures. Remember that the Savior felt rejection from people he loved. Elder Orson F. Whitney taught:

> No pain that we suffer, no trial that we experience is wasted. It ministers to our education, to the development of such qualities as patience, faith, fortitude, and humility. All that we suffer and all that we endure, especially when we endure it patiently, builds up our characters, purifies our hearts, expands our souls, and makes us more tender and charitable, more worthy to be called the children of God. (As quoted in Spencer W. Kimball, *Faith Precedes the Miracle* [Salt Lake City: Deseret Book, 1972], p. 98)

Our Father in Heaven has interesting ways of giving us a caring heart. Having gone through a few difficult breakups myself, I know I look at others going through the same experience much differently than I used to. My heart aches with empathy. Sometimes all I can do is be a listening ear. At least I'm now wise enough to know that I shouldn't walk up and ignorantly suggest, "C'mon, get over it!" or "Don't worry, be happy!"

To someone who's never been through a bad breakup, a few of the suggestions above may sound strange or perhaps even silly. But we're not talking about what's logical or sensible. We're talking about survival!

One time, while going through this healing process, I saw a bumper sticker that said, "Since I gave up hope, I feel much better." Oddly enough, taking this attitude (not permanently, of course, but just for a few days) felt kind of good. It was another way of saying, "I'm going to focus on things I can control for a while." It's like a test question that you leave blank, knowing that when you get some other questions done you'll come back to it. So just "bag it" for now, and eventually you'll be ready to jump back into the dating game again.

In time, your feelings of hope and anticipation will return. One thing I know for sure: whenever I thought to myself, "Where will I find another like her?" *I always did!* And you will too.

If You Did the Breaking Off

It's difficult to know which is harder, getting "dumped" or feeling it necessary to "dump" someone else. Inevitably, when there is a breakup, one person is hurt worse than the other. It's awful to know that you've hurt someone's feelings. When you tell someone you just want to be friends, it's not like saying, "I don't like your shirt," or "I don't like the way you drive." You're saying, "I don't like *you*." At least, that's how it feels to the other person. Ouch. That's hard.

I remember a time in my life that's still hard for me to think about, a time when I hurt someone's feelings pretty badly. She was a wonderful person, and I felt horrible, but I knew it was not right. I ached. I kept telling myself, I was not sent to earth to hurt people! I just didn't want to date anymore if this was what was going to happen.

I remember one Sunday when I was praying very earnestly for this girl, a bit of inspiration came my way. It was as if the Lord was saying to me, "Don't worry. She's my daughter. There is nothing you can teach me about how to take care of my children." This helped me to realize that she too was being watched over by her Heavenly Father, and she would be okay.

If you're in a situation like this, here's some advice: When you break up, break up! Because you may still have concern for the other person, you may be tempted to keep in touch. Sometimes it's better to disappear. It may not be possible to go from being in a romantic relationship to being "just friends." And although you want to call each day and say, "How are you doing today?" it may be better to leave it alone.

On either side of an ending relationship, it's common to ask, "Why did I have to go through this?" Good question. Welcome to life, I guess. Whether there is a specific purpose for each of our trials, I don't know. But I do know that we can always find things to learn through our hard times.

In my student ward, we had a high councilor who didn't marry until he was in his forties. He always used to say:

> *The wrong one*
> *Is the right one*
> *To lead you*
> *To the best one.*

I believe there are things we can learn from all of our trials, even our failed relationships. We can always find lessons on ways we can be better people and friends.

Measure Your Self-Worth by How the Lord Sees You

After a bad breakup, it's common for people to experience a real crisis in their feelings about themselves. They ask questions like, "What's wrong with me?" "Why wasn't I good enough?" "Why would anyone want me in the future?"

Sometimes we may make the mistake of attaching all of our self-worth to someone else. We can be happy only if they like us, and if they decide they don't, we are devastated. How someone feels about us will naturally have an impact on our feelings, but we need to be sure to keep it in perspective. Basing our self-worth on how others treat us is a false and dangerous system.

It's important to realize that just because a relationship failed, that doesn't mean you're not a worthwhile person. I love ketchup, and I love caramel sauce, but I don't mix them and pour them together on ice cream. They're fine individually; they just don't do well together. In the same way, both of you may be fine, wonderful individuals, but the combination just doesn't work.

The only real, enduring way to have appropriate feelings of self-worth is in the gospel. The scriptures offer many interesting examples: Nephi called himself a "wretched man" because he at times felt anger toward his brothers. In the end, however, Nephi said, "I know in whom I have trusted. My God hath been my support" (2 Nephi 4:17, 19–20). Ammon said, "I will not boast of myself, but I will boast of my God, for in his strength I can do all things" (Alma 26:12). Ammon recognized the source of his power. Moses had the privilege of seeing and conversing with God, and when the presence of the Lord withdrew from him, he said, "Now . . . I know that man is nothing, which thing I never had supposed" (Moses 1:10). When Satan approached Moses and said, "Moses, son of man, worship me," Moses responded beautifully: "Who art thou? For behold, I am a son of God" (Moses 1:12–13). Moses was *dependent* on God, but he also knew he was a *descendant* of God. Appropriate feelings of self-worth fall somewhere in this combination of recognizing our own nothingness and understanding our divine potential. The idea is not necessarily to have confidence in ourselves, but to have confidence and faith in God that he can make us into something wonderful.

Brother Stephen R. Covey told of an object lesson he taught his students. He asked them to fold a piece of paper in half lengthwise and then open it up so it had two columns. In the first column, they were to write what other people thought of them. If others thought they were weird, odd, ugly, or unattractive, they were to write it down. In the second column, they were to write what God thought about them. What do you suppose they wrote?

All our lives we've heard prophets describe the valiance of the youth of the last days. We've learned how the Savior has loved us, and we often reflect on what we must be worth as we remember the lines of the hymn "I Stand All Amazed": "Oh it is wonderful that he should care for me enough to die for me." We find clues in our patriarchal blessings as we look at our lineage and our capacities and possibilities. When Brother Covey's students were all finished with their two columns, he asked them an interesting question: "Which side are you going to believe?"

The world uses several false systems that don't work. Fame and popularity don't guarantee happiness. Wealth and accomplishments won't work either. Relying on what other people think of us is dangerous because people are fickle.

If you've been through a bad breakup, stay close to the Lord. He knows what you are worth, and he is the Master Healer. Build your foundation on him, because he is the rock, the only sure foundation. And this rock will never break up (see Helaman 5:12).

Bottom line: breakups are a part of life for everyone. They're hard. They hurt. But they can teach us empathy and make us better people in the long run. Learn what you can, be patient with yourself as you heal, and keep the faith. Just don't let breakups break you up.

Indian Love Poem

Nice night
in June
Stars shine
Big moon.
In park
on bench
with girl
In clinch.
Me say
"Me love"
She coo
Like dove.
Me smart
Me fast
Never let
Chance pass.
"Get hitched,"
Me say
She say
"Okay."
Wedding bells
Ring ring
Honeymoon
Everything
Settle down

Married life
Everything
Happy life.
*

'Nother night
In June
Stars shine
Big moon.
No happy
No more
Carry baby
Walk floor.
Wife mad
She fuss
Me mad
Me cuss.
Life one
Big spat
Naggy wife
Bawling brat.
Me see
At last—
Me too
Darn fast.

—Author unknown

WHEN DO YOU SEEK MARRIAGE?

I'm getting married in the morning!
—Eliza Doolittle's father

I'VE NEVER SEEN ANYTHING from the Church that gives a recommended age for marrying. But I have heard counsel that marriage should be neither rushed into nor deliberately postponed. President Gordon B. Hinckley has taught:

> I do not worry very much about the young men and women, including many returned missionaries, who are of such an age that in all likelihood they will be married within a relatively short time. I feel they should not be put under pressure by counsel from Church leaders to rush into it. But neither do I believe that they should dally along in a fruitless, frustrating, and frivolous dating game that only raises hopes and brings disappointment and in some cases heartache. (*Teachings of Gordon B. Hinckley* [Salt Lake City: Deseret Book, 1997], p. 603)

For a long time, as a young adult, I wondered why people kept coming up to my piano and asking me with such urgency, "When are you going to play that duet?" (They obviously saw my receding hairline and figured that time was running out.) I've always understood why marriage was *important*, but why is it *urgent*? Well, I've done some asking and thinking and reading and more asking, and here's what I've come up with. (This isn't from the Church, it's just my list.)

1. Longer exposure to temptation and the desires of the flesh increases the possibility of moral transgression.

President Ezra Taft Benson said: "The plaguing sin of this generation is sexual immorality. This, the Prophet Joseph said, would be the source of more temptations, more buffetings, and more difficulties for the elders of Israel than any other. (See *Journal of Discourses* 8:55.)"

2. Important knowledge and growth needed to become more like God can be acquired best in a family setting, as a spouse and a parent.

Nothing could have prepared me for the feeling I had when the doctor handed me my new baby girl. I had a new understanding of the word *father* that I could not have learned from reading books. My love, empathy, and concern for my little girl grows daily. In a small way, I'm learning how our Father in Heaven must feel about us, and what it meant for him to send his Son.

Elder John H. Groberg taught: "We come to this earth charged with a mission: to learn to love and serve one another. To best help us accomplish this, God has placed us in families, for he knows that is where we can best learn to overcome selfishness and pride and to sacrifice for others and to make happiness and helpfulness and humility and love the very essence of our character" (*Ensign*, May 1982, p. 50).

3. Marriage is an ordinance!

Not only is marriage a commandment but it's also an ordinance. It is urgent that we move along the path that leads to exaltation. If we have been baptized and received our endowment, the next step along the path would be to participate in the ordinance of celestial marriage.

Elder Bruce R. McConkie wrote:

> The most important things that any member of The Church of Jesus Christ of Latter-day Saints ever does in this world are: 1. To marry the right person, in the right place, by the right authority; and 2. To keep the covenant made in connection with this holy and perfect order of matrimony—thus assuring the obedient persons of an inheritance of exaltation in the celestial kingdom. (*Mormon Doctrine*, 2nd ed. [Salt Lake City: Bookcraft, 1966], p. 118)

The Doctrine and Covenants tells that marriage is essential to exaltation:

> In the celestial glory there are three heavens or degrees;
> And in order to obtain the highest, a man must enter into this order of the priesthood [meaning the new and everlasting covenant of marriage];
> And if he does not, he cannot obtain it.
> He may enter into the other, but that is the end of his kingdom; he cannot have an increase. (D&C 131:1–4)

4. *The longer one remains single, the less available are potential spouses of similar age.*

This is the one that used to keep me up at night. Marriage is urgent because, as you grow older, there are fewer individuals of marriageable age from whom to choose.

5. *The biological clock keeps ticking for men and women.*

Parenthood requires energy and time. You will want to be able to have as many children as the Lord would like you to have without endangering your health. Marriage is urgent because it's tough to have the energy you need to have teenagers at home when you're in your eighties.

6. *It's a better way to live!*

This is the happiest reason of all. Being married is simply a better way to live. The Lord said, "It is not good that the man should be alone" (Genesis 2:18). Why is it not good? Because there's something better. President Spencer W. Kimball taught, "While marriage is difficult, and discordant and frustrated marriages are common, yet real, lasting happiness is possible, and marriage can be more an exultant ecstasy than the human mind can conceive" (*Teachings of Spencer W. Kimball*, pp. 305–6). Elder James E. Faust expressed a similar feeling this way: "Happiness in marriage and parenthood can exceed a thousand times any other happiness" (*Ensign*, November 1977, p. 11).

It's no good to be married just for the sake of being married, though. Elder Marvin J. Ashton taught, "We must ever realize that being single will never be as painful as being married to the wrong person with wrong and selfish standards" (Single Member Fireside, 30 August 1992).

So here's the ranking for the best way to do life:

1. Happily Married
2. Happily Single
3. Bitterly Single (because at least you're still single, and have your options open)
4. Unhappily Married

So, why the rush to get you to the church on time? When you were a little kid who used to run around the house screaming, your parents let you do it because they thought you needed to get some of your energy out. After a while, they figured you'd had enough time to mess around, so they turned to you and said, "Hey, would you settle down?"

Now you're older. You're graduating from high school and getting into college or serving a mission. Just what you need to get some energy out. Once you start getting into your twenties, you'll hear it again, "Hey, when are you going to settle down?" Settling down is what it's all about. It's about opening new doors with more opportunities for growth and learning. It's about getting down to the business of fulfilling one of the major purposes of earth life: *making eternal families.*

The following questions appear in the Foundations for Temple Marriage Teacher's Manual *(Salt Lake City: The Church of Jesus Christ of Latter-day Saints, 1979), p. 46.*

- *How do your and your potential spouse's interests compare in occupations, parents, friends, church callings, educational pursuits, and hobbies?*
- *Have you both learned to exchange suggestions for improvement in your relationship without giving or taking offense?*
- *How do you now make decisions that affect the both of you? After marriage, who will be "boss"? Will the husband be "head of the house," and, if so, how will he preside as a patriarch? Will he be able to counsel and plan with his wife? To respect her opinions? To consider her needs?*
- *Have you gone together long enough to see each other in a variety of social settings? Has your relationship changed over the course of time? Has it improved?*
- *Have you associated with each other's family enough to know the background of your potential marriage partner? How can or will your parents enhance your marriage once you are married? Are there any potential in-law problems?*
- *How will the money be managed once it is earned? Who will pay the bills and/or keep the checkbook? Do you have similar expectations about the use of credit, savings, or debt? To what degree are you committed to tithing and other financial offerings in The Church of Jesus Christ of Latter-day Saints?*
- *After marriage are either or both of you going to seek additional occupational training or education? Have adequate financial plans been made for these plans?*
- *Will the wife attend or complete college? Do either of you plan for her to work after marriage? After children are born?*
- *Have you discussed having children? How many do you want and when? Who will care for, tend, and discipline them after they are born?*
- *Are you both knowledgeable about running an orderly home? What do you consider to be the woman's role? The man's role?*
- *Do either of you have excessive fears or anxieties about the sexual relationship in marriage? Are you both willing to wait until marriage and then express physical or sexual intimacies only in marriage?*

WHOM SHOULD YOU MARRY?

I wanted to evoke the joys of childhood and being in love
when I created the title number from Singin' in the Rain.
. . . I wanted to bring audiences back to their childhoods
when they would cavort in the rain, even though their
mothers would give them trouble. . . . I also wanted to
make them feel like they were in love. A fellow in love
does silly things.
—Gene Kelly

WHOM SHOULD YOU MARRY? Well, the short answer to that question is that you should marry the one you choose. That was less of a problem for Adam and Eve, but for everyone else, everything I've read from Church leaders seems to indicate that *you* have the responsibility to choose the one you want to marry, then ask the Lord for his approval.

Properly understood, the teachings of the gospel concerning courtship and marriage are a great source of counsel and comfort. However, our lack of a correct understanding of certain doctrines and principles can also become a source of confusion. A couple of common misunderstandings would include (1) that a spouse has already been assigned to us, and we must ask the Lord to tell us whom to marry, and (2) that others can receive revelations for us about whom we should marry. Elder Bruce R. McConkie taught:

> How do you choose a wife? I've heard a lot of young people from Brigham Young University and elsewhere say, "I've got to get a feeling of inspiration. I've got to get some revelation. I've got to fast and pray and get the Lord to manifest to me whom I should marry." Well, maybe it will be a little shock to you, but never in my life did I ask the Lord whom I ought to marry. It never occurred to me to ask him. I went out and found the girl I wanted; she suited me; I evaluated and weighed the proposition, and it just seemed a hundred percent to me as though this ought to be. Now, if I'd done things perfectly, I'd have done some counseling with the Lord, which I didn't do; but all I did was pray to the Lord and ask for some guidance and direction in connection with the decision that I'd reached. A more perfect thing to have done would have been to counsel with him relative to the decision and get a spiritual confirmation that the conclusion, which I by my agency and faculties had arrived at, was the right one. ("Agency or Inspiration?" *New Era*, January 1975, p. 40)

If we believe that someone else has already chosen a spouse for us, we make someone else responsible for our decision and hence for the success of our union. With this misunderstanding, some people who marry and then have marital problems may assume, "Well, I guess I married the wrong one."

President Boyd K. Packer taught:

> Righteous love comes so naturally and so beautifully that it is apparent that there is a special providence about it. "They were meant for each other," we say. While I am sure some young couples have some special guidance in getting together, I do not believe in predestined love. If you desire the inspiration of the Lord in this crucial decision, you must live the standards of the Church, and you must pray constantly for the wisdom to recognize those qualities upon which a successful union may be based. You must do the choosing, rather than to seek for some one-and-only so-called soul mate, chosen for you by someone else and waiting for you. You are to do the choosing. You must be wise beyond your years and humbly prayerful lest you choose amiss. *(Eternal Love,* p. 11)

Related to this idea of every person having a "one and only" would be the problem of someone making a mistake. If only one person chose the "wrong one," the domino effect would cause all of us to choose wrong! During the 1970s, an unofficial Church-related musical gave many well-meaning Latter-day Saints the impression that we made premortal covenants with our spouses-to-be. The "I Have a Question" section of the June 1977 *Ensign* included this query: "Is it true that each of us contracted with someone during our premortal lives to find and marry that person here?" The response quotes the First Presidency saying, "We have no revealed word to the effect that when we were in the preexistent state we chose our parents and our husbands and wives."

It also quotes President Joseph Fielding Smith, "It is possible that in some instances it is true, but it would require too great a stretch of the imagination to believe it in all, or even in the majority of cases." The article continues:

> This idea seems to assume that prior to mortality we knew everyone we would meet on earth well enough to make that kind of decision. Some of us made promises as childhood sweethearts that in maturity were wisely never kept. The same may be true for premortal sweethearts, if there are such. One young lady, when informed by a returned missionary that she made a premortal covenant to marry him, replied, "Even if I made that mistake there, I am not going to make it here." Since we should be making spiritual progress here, and since covenants only have eternal validity if sealed by the Spirit (D&C 132:7), perhaps some of us can make better marriage choices in mortality. (*Ensign,* June 1977, p. 40)

As I understand the subject from my studies, it seems that the Lord allows and expects us to make our own choice concerning someone to marry. The idea that we're "supposed" to marry someone (whether we want to or not) contradicts the principle of agency. Everything I've read seems to indicate that we seek the Lord's approval of the decision we've already made, not that we ask the Lord whom we're "supposed" to marry.

Why Did We Get Different Answers?

Some interesting dilemmas can arise from a righteous desire to follow the Spirit. For example, perhaps a couple is having a lot of problems; this confuses them because they thought they received an answer to prayer concerning their relationship. I've appreciated this explanation from Brother Gawain Wells:

> Some couples may argue that they received a spiritual confirmation of their relationship. Why, then, didn't it work out? It's possible, of course, that you wanted so badly for it to work out that you misinterpreted spiritual feelings and, in essence, put words in God's mouth. But there's another possibility: People change. Though the dating relationship was right at one time, it isn't anymore. The spiritual confirmation could have been an assurance of the relationship's capacity, its possibility, its potential. But it wasn't a guarantee of ultimate fruit. ("Breaking Up without Going to Pieces," *Ensign*, June 1982, pp. 58–61)

Here's another common one. Perhaps one person felt that he or she received a "yes" answer, but the other got a "no." Should one person rely on the other's spirituality and follow whatever answer that person says? Elder Dallin H. Oaks taught:

> I have heard of cases where a young man told a young woman she should marry him because he had received a revelation that she was to be his eternal companion. If this is a true revelation, it will be confirmed directly to the woman if she seeks to know. In the meantime, she is under no obligation to heed it. . . . The man can receive revelation to guide his own actions, but he cannot properly receive

revelation to direct hers. She is outside his stewardship. ("Revelation," *BYU 1981–82 Fireside and Devotional Speeches*, p. 25)

Brother Gerald N. Lund, speaking at a Church Educational System fireside for young adults, made a similar statement:

> When I was teaching in the institutes of religion in Southern California, there was hardly a semester that went by that I didn't have an experience like this: One of my students would come to me (usually a girl) and report that the boy she had been dating (sometimes seriously, sometimes casually) had received a "revelation" that they were to marry. I won't ask for a show of hands how many here have faced a similar declaration, but I know, from my own experience, it will be more than a few of you. Carlfred Broderick, a renowned LDS family therapist, dubbed these as "hormonal revelations" (Carlfred Broderick, *One Flesh, One Heart: Putting Celestial Love into Your Temple Marriage*, Salt Lake City: Deseret Book, 1986, p. 21).
>
> The interesting thing to me was that often the girl felt intimidated by such a declaration, feeling that she needed to accept the "Lord's will" even though she found the prospect somewhat distasteful. (In some cases it was downright distasteful.) Some were even a little shocked when I boldly explained that unless they received an independent confirmation from the Lord, they should feel no pressure to accept the boy's request. (*Speeches, 1997–98*

[Provo, Utah: Brigham Young University, 1998], pp. 81–82)

A young woman might say, "Well, since he got an answer, and because he has the priesthood, I guess that's the Lord's will, and I want to follow the Lord's will." One of the most sobering stories I've heard on this subject was in a talk given by Bruce C. Hafen:

> Some years ago, a young couple planning a temple marriage came to my office here at BYU (I was in a student stake presidency) for recommend interviews. At the conclusion of my private interview with the young woman, I asked if she had any questions. She said, "Well, yes, there is one question: Is it all right to marry someone if you don't love them?" That puzzled me more than mildly since she was planning to be sealed in the temple in just a few days. We talked a little further. She told me the story of their courtship, when after fasting and prayer, she had been unable to feel that she should marry this young man, he told her he felt the proposed marriage had the Lord's approval. Then she told me she was a recent convert to the Church, and had great respect for the priesthood. So, she said, "He and I both decided that because he held the priesthood, he had the authority to receive the correct answer to my prayer. And now I'm willing to marry him if that's what I'm supposed to do. But in all honesty I must admit I don't love him . . ."
>
> That was a very difficult time for me. But I felt that I should talk to the young man alone,

which I did. I tried to explain to him that as I understood the teachings of the Church, he had no priesthood authority over this girl, as much as he loved her and in spite of his great intentions and hopes for them. I asked him if he knew her true feelings, and then I suggested the two of them might want to talk a little further to be sure of themselves. As far as I know they never did marry. This experience left me wondering how intelligent members of the Church could become so confused about the role of priesthood authority. ("Women, Feminism, and the Priesthood," audiocassette [Provo, Utah: BYU Media Services, 1985])

This might be a good time to express a little thought: If you really don't want to marry someone, that's probably a good sign that you shouldn't. (You might want to jot that one down somewhere.)

What If I Get No Answer?

Sometimes receiving no answer *is* an answer. In our efforts to do what's right, we might say, "I'll do whatever I need to do, just tell me." That's a righteous desire, but it's a little like saying to your fireplace, "Give me heat, and then I'll give you wood." You have to do the work before you get the benefit. You'll notice that when Nephi and his brothers were trying to get the brass plates from Laban, their first two attempts failed. As Nephi began his third attempt, he didn't say, "Lord, I'm not moving until you tell me exactly what to do." Rather, he said, "And I was led by the Spirit, *not knowing beforehand* the things which I should do" (1 Nephi 4:6; emphasis added). This was a real test of faith, and Nephi proceeded without knowing for sure what would happen.

Elder Marion G. Romney taught, "While the Lord will magnify us in both subtle and dramatic ways, he can only guide our footsteps when we move our feet" (*Ensign*, May 1981, p. 91). Perhaps it is more common to receive the absence of a "no" answer than it is to receive a "yes" answer. Elder John H. Groberg has said:

> In the past I have tried to figure out whether I should go into business or into teaching or into the arts or whatever. As I have begun to proceed along one path, having more or less gathered what facts I could, I have found that if that decision was wrong or was taking me down the wrong path—not necessarily an evil one, but one that was not right for me—without fail, the Lord has always let me know just this emphatically: "That is wrong; do not go that way. That is not for you!"
>
> On the other hand, there may have been two or three ways that I could have gone, any one of which would have been right and would have been in the general area providing the experience and means whereby I could fulfill the mission that the Lord had in mind for me. Because he knows we need the growth, he generally does not point and say, "Open that door and go twelve yards in that direction; then turn right and go two miles. . . ." But if that is wrong, he will let us know—we will feel it for sure. I am positive of that. So rather than saying, "I will not move until I have this burning in my heart," let us turn it around and say, "I will

move unless I feel it is wrong; and if it is wrong, I will not do it." By eliminating all of these wrong courses, very quickly you will find yourself going in the direction that you ought to be going, and then you can receive the assurance: "Yes, I am going in the right direction. I am doing what my Father in Heaven wants me to do because I am not doing the things he does not want me to do." And you can know that for sure. That is part of the growth process and part of accomplishing what our Father in Heaven has in mind for us. ("What Is Your Mission?" *BYU Speeches of the Year, 1979*, pp. 97–98)

The Lord told Oliver Cowdery to "study it out in [his] mind" before making a decision (D&C 9:8). I suppose we have to do our homework and then take our best shot. Once committed to a course of action, we are more likely to receive the guidance we desire. Brother Joseph Fielding McConkie told of a young woman who had to make a decision in order to receive an answer:

A young woman received a proposal from a fine young man she had been dating. Uncertain in her feelings and unable to identify a clear spiritual direction, she sought counsel with her bishop. He explained that he could not and would not attempt to make that decision for her, but suggested that if she committed herself to a course of action, she would almost immediately find it confirmed or hedged up with feelings of foreboding. She went back to the young man and told him that she would marry him. With that commitment came a feeling as though she had been immersed in a sea of darkness. The engagement lasted twenty-four hours. She later suggested that she could not conceive a more dramatic or emphatic answer to her prayers and that she was extremely grateful for it, notwithstanding the temporary embarrassment associated with it. (*The Spirit of Revelation* [Salt Lake City: Deseret Book, 1984], p. 37)

I feel confident that the Lord will not leave us alone in making this major decision, and we can expect to be guided, even if we don't realize it at the time. I have also learned that when we do our best, the Lord will honor our effort. President Brigham Young taught:

If I do not know the will of my Father, and what he requires of me in a certain transaction, if I ask Him to give me wisdom concerning any requirement in life, or in regard to my own course, or that of my friends, my family, my children, or those that I preside over, and get no answer from Him, and then do the very best that my judgment will teach me, He is bound to own and honor that transaction, and He will do so to all intents and purposes. (*Journal of Discourses*, 26 vols. [London: Latter-day Saints' Book Depot, 1854–1886], 3:205)

These spiritual guidance issues are difficult. Learning to receive and recognize answers to our prayers may be a lifelong struggle, and my printing a list of interesting quotes may not be enough to answer all of your questions. When seeking guidance about the marriage decision, many young adults will second-guess, third-guess, and fourth-guess themselves about their spiritual feelings. When you receive an answer, your mind will often come up with an alternative explanation. You may ask, "Am I experiencing a stupor of thought, or is Satan just trying to make me feel bad about a good thing?" Or, "Did I receive an approval from the Lord, or was I just feeling what I hoped I would feel?" Sometimes you just have to do the best you know how, trust God, and move forward with faith.

Another danger is to expect things to happen for you the same way they did for your friends. I personally know married couples who felt they received an answer about their relationship when they were dating, others when they were engaged, and some who didn't receive confirmation of their decision until *after* they were married! As President Boyd K. Packer has taught, we can't force spiritual things or dictate to the Lord when or how he should answer us (see *That All May Be Edified* [Salt Lake City: Bookcraft, 1982], p. 338).

I believe that these things often work out not *because* of our efforts, but *in spite* of them. There have been many times in my life when I felt like I was receiving no help from the Lord at all, so I just had to take my best shot and move on. A few months later, I would look back and realize that I was being guided all along. The most important thing, I suppose, is to strive to remain worthy and available to the Spirit of the Lord so that you can be guided even if you don't realize it at the time. Bruce C. Hafen taught:

> In general, remember that you will need— as much as you will ever need it for any

purpose—the guidance of the Holy Ghost in seeking an eternal companion and in building relationships toward that end. The key to spiritual guidance is not how long you pray, or what steps of prayer you follow, or what words you say. The key to spiritual guidance is found in one word: worthiness. ("The Gospel and Romantic Love," *Ensign,* October 1982, p. 68)

Well, we've talked about some of the spiritual guidance issues, but what about basic compatibility? While it's clear that the Lord wants us to do the choosing, it's also clear that we should choose wisely. Elder Mark E. Petersen said, "Enough difficulties develop in the best of marriages to convince us that we should take as few problems to the altar as we can" ("Selecting Your Mate," in *Marriage and Common Sense* [Salt Lake City: Bookcraft, 1972], p. 11).

A temple sealing is a wonderful event, but it doesn't automatically change personalities or dispositions. The same people who walk into the sealing room walk out. Sometimes people are so excited about the wedding that they forget about the marriage. It reminds me of the story of the new bride who said to her mother, "Oh, Mom, I'm so happy! I'm at the end of my troubles." To which the mother replied, "Yes, but which end?" The excitement and glamour of the wedding day end quickly; then real life together begins. If you're planning to spend the rest of your life together with someone, the choice of that person is not a decision to be made in an instant. You may have many qualities on your wish list. Here are a few that I like: marry someone you're attracted to inside and out, marry your best friend, and marry someone you love.

Marry Someone You're Attracted To Inside and Out

Physical attractiveness in a potential mate is just the *beginning* of the list. If you went by the example of those in Hollywood, it would be the *whole* list. Unfortunately, we live in a society that has taught us to appreciate very few body types. Not all of us will look like a supermodel or an athlete. When you're looking for someone to marry, certainly there should be some physical attraction, but don't get the package mixed up with the contents.

Back when I was just a pup, there was a TV game show called *Let's Make a Deal*. Contestants would have to choose between what was behind curtain number one or what was hidden beneath a beautifully wrapped box. Sometimes the wrapping was deceiving. Underneath the colorful ribbons and bows might be a couple of bricks, a pig, or a tin bucket. On other occasions it could be cash or expensive jewelry. (You know where I'm going with this, don't you?) A person's wrapping tells very little about what's inside. If you're looking only for good looks, charm, and a nice car, you're looking for a prom date, not a spouse.

This is not to say that you should go out and find the most unattractive person possible. Certainly you want to be attracted to your spouse. President Ezra Taft Benson listed attractiveness as one of the qualities to look for, but not at the expense of many others. Speaking to the single adult men of the Church, he said:

> Now, brethren, do not expect perfection in your choice of a mate. Do not be so particular that you overlook her most important qualities

of having a strong testimony, living the principles of the gospel, loving home, wanting to be a mother in Zion, and supporting you in your priesthood responsibilities.

Of course, she should be attractive to you, but do not just date one girl after another for the sole pleasure of dating without seeking the Lord's confirmation in your choice of your eternal companion. ("To the Single Adult Brethren of the Church," *Ensign,* May 1988, p. 53)

Yes, being attracted to the one you want to marry is important, but you will also find that a person's appearance changes the more you get to know him or her. We have all known very attractive or handsome people who have lost some of their appeal when their personality showed them inside to be unkind or clique-ish. We have also known average-looking people to become quite attractive when their interaction with others revealed their kindness and goodness. When you really love someone for what's inside, that person will remain attractive to you forever. I have been touched by these words of President Gordon B. Hinckley:

May I be personal for a moment? I sat at dinner across the table from my wife the other evening. It was fifty-five years ago that we were married in the Salt Lake Temple. The wondrous aura of young womanhood was upon her. She was beautiful, and I was bewitched. Now, for more than half a century, we have walked together through much of storm as well as sunshine. Today neither of us stands as tall as we once did. As I looked at her across the table, I noted a few wrinkles in her face and hands. But are they less beautiful than before? No, in fact, they are more so. Those wrinkles have a beauty of their own, and inherent in their very presence is something that speaks reassuringly of strength and integrity and a love that runs more deeply and quietly than ever before. ("This I Believe," *BYU 1991–92 Devotional and Fireside Speeches*, March 1, 1992, p. 78)

I believe that attractiveness has much more to do with the personality of a person than the appearance. Once you are a married couple, daily experiencing the ups and downs of life, you will see how little appearance matters to a happy marriage. A happy disposition, on the other hand, will make your spouse more beautiful than ever. So, by all means, marry someone you are attracted to. Just make sure the prize on the inside matches the wrapping on the outside.

Marry Your Best Friend

One night, while munching on Jordan almonds at a wedding reception, I noticed the printing on the commemorative napkins: "Today I Marry My Best Friend." I wanted to take out a pen and add, "Because what kind of an idiot would marry someone they couldn't stand?" It seemed rather obvious to me that you should marry someone you liked, but I guess there's a reason they don't add my additional comment.

"Marry your best friend" may sound like a cliché, but it's good advice (unless your name is Frank and your best friend is Bill). It's important to marry someone you love, but it's also important to marry someone you like.

In other words, you *like* being together, you *like* to do the same things, you *like* each other. You're friends! Romance may have ups and downs, but friendship endures. Elder Marion D. Hanks taught:

> Married people should be *best friends;* no relationship on earth needs friendship as much as marriage. . . . Friendship in a marriage is so important. It blows away the chaff and takes the kernel, rejoices in the uniqueness of each the other, listens patiently, gives generously, forgives freely. Friendship will motivate one to cross the room one day and say, "I'm sorry. I didn't mean that." It will not pretend perfection, or demand it. It will not insist that both respond exactly the same in every thought and feeling, but it will bring to the union honesty, integrity. There will be repentance and forgiveness in every marriage—every good marriage—and respect and trust. (*Ensign,* November 1984, p. 36)

I think one of the best signs of a good and growing friendship is the ability to talk without much effort. I've been on lots of dates where I couldn't think of a single thing to say. It wasn't fun, it was work! I came home exhausted. You can talk about the weather for only so long. By contrast, I was on a date once where the waiter had to come back to our table three times for our order. We had so much to talk about, we kept forgetting to look at the menu.

Paul E. Dahl, an institute director, wrote:

> Recently a woman in our town, who had been a wife for forty-two years, stated that she

and her husband were "terribly good friends" and had a tremendous amount of respect for each other. She said this greatly strengthened their relationship because they always had something to talk about. They understood each other and were interested in each other. Too often we think that friendships are something external to marriage, but it is my experience that a really happy and healthy marriage is based on a solid friendship. ("Keeping Your Marriage Alive," *Ensign*, July 1982, p. 59)

We often use the term *intimacy* to describe this quality of friendship, referring not to a physical kind of intimacy, but to the feeling of emotional closeness and connection. This type of intimacy in a marriage is priceless. C. Richard Chidester, an institute instructor, wrote:

In intimate relationships, we share feelings we normally keep hidden—doubts and fears, joys and sorrows, hopes and dreams. Most people marry out of a hunger for intimacy, but few achieve it. In fact, I feel that a great deal of suffering and loneliness in relationships can be traced back to a lack of intimacy. ("Keeping in Touch with Feelings," *Ensign*, July 1979, p. 15)

Without this type of intimacy, you may be tempted to look elsewhere for friendship. Elder Hugh W. Pinnock counseled:

Remember never to turn to a third party in time of marital trouble except to your bishop or branch president. . . . Someone is always ready and eager to consult a hurting wife or husband, and when marriage partners have no one to talk with at home, unfortunately, too often they seek a friend elsewhere. And that, dear brothers and sisters, is where almost all adultery has its origin. ("Ten Keys to Successful Dating and Marriage Relationships," *BYU Fireside and Devotional Speeches, 1981,* p. 75)

Whom should you marry? Marry your best friend—someone you enjoy being with even when you're not sharing affection. Someone with whom you can spend the whole day and never feel bored or lonely. Someone who is the first person you want to tell when something exciting happens to you. Someone you really like.

Marry Someone You Love

For a long time as a young adult, I looked for definitions of "falling in love." I wanted to fall in love, and I wanted to know what it felt like. I didn't want Hollywood's definition; I wanted one I could trust. Some of my questions included: Can you choose to fall in love with someone? Is falling in love a spiritual feeling? Does growing older diminish your ability to fall in love? Would it be improper to ask Heavenly Father to *make* someone fall in love with me?

I entered my dating years with the head-in-the-clouds definition of falling in love. That's the euphoric, I-want-to-hug-everyone feeling that all the songs on the radio are about. And to be sure, it's real—the feeling, that is. And it is *wonderful.* But over the years I've learned that it's not real love. Some of us mistake this feeling for real love, and we end up "falling in love with love." Ever done that? Me too. Loving a person is not the same thing as being in love with love. President Spencer W. Kimball described the difference:

> What is love? Many people think of it as mere physical attraction and they casually speak of "falling in love" and "love at first sight." This may be Hollywood's version and the interpretation of those who write love songs and love fiction. True love is not wrapped in such flimsy material. One might become immediately attracted to another individual, but love is far more than physical attraction. It is deep, inclusive and comprehensive. Physical attraction is only one of the many elements; there must be faith and confidence and understanding and partnership. There must be common ideals and standards. There must be great devotion and companionship. *Love is cleanliness and progress and sacrifice and selflessness.* This kind of love never tires or wanes, but lives through sickness and sorrow, poverty and privation, accomplishment and disappointment, time and eternity. For the love to continue, there must be an increase constantly of confidence and understanding, of frequent and sincere expression of appreciation and affection. There must be a forgetting of self and a constant concern for the other. Interests, hopes, objectives must be constantly focused into a single channel. (*Faith Precedes the Miracle* [Salt Lake City: Deseret Book, 1972], pp. 157–58; emphasis added)

When a teenage girl looks across the dance floor and squeals with delight, "Oh, he's so gorgeous!" that's definitely a feeling, but it's not real love. On the big screen, when eyes meet across a crowded room and the music swells, that's a feeling too. But on such an occasion, you don't hear the actors say, "Wow, suddenly I'm filled with cleanliness, progress, sacrifice, and selflessness." Real love is, "I'll take the baby for a while; you go take a nap." Real love is, "I'll be out with the car, can I get you anything?" Real love is, "Wow, I guess it was something you ate. . . . I'll clean it off the carpet; you go lie down." They don't show that part in the movies.

One day my elders quorum president gave me a book to read. You can always tell what people think of you by the titles of the books they give you. This one was called *How to Stop Looking for Someone Perfect and Find Someone to Love* (New York: Ballantine Books, 1984). The author, Judith Sills, was not a member of the Church, but I sensed the truth in what she had to say:

> The question of love—that's love as in "Am I in love?" or "I still love her but I'm not in love" or "I want desperately to be in love"—is the central source of confusion in the selection of a mate.
>
> "In love" is, by definition and strong preference, an irrational state. It is also temporary, though it can cycle through a long relationship. It is odd that people seek out a period of temporary insanity as the ideal mind-set for making a crucial life decision. It would be sensible to say, "I can't decide whether to marry you or not. I'm too much in love to think clearly." Instead, people often feel that if they are not in

the grip of this madness something vital is lacking. (P. 51)

I knew that I couldn't trust the euphoric, high-school infatuation feelings, because I'd felt them over girls who later turned out to be totally wrong for me. I also knew that Bruce C. Hafen said you could fall in love with someone you shouldn't marry. Eventually, I came across a couple of definitions of being in love that I liked. They made sense to my mind, and they felt good to my spirit. One was from President David O. McKay, and the other was from President Ezra Taft Benson.

> "How may I know when I am in love?" That is a very important question. A fellow student and I considered that query one night as we walked together. As boys of that age frequently do, we were talking about girls. Neither he nor I knew whether or not we were in love. Of course I had not then met my present sweetheart. In answer to my question, "How may we know when we are in love?" he replied: "My mother once said that if you meet a girl in whose presence you feel a desire to achieve, who inspires you to do your best, and to make the most of yourself, such a young woman is worthy of your love and is awakening love in your heart." I submit that as a true guide. (David O. McKay, *Gospel Ideals* [Salt Lake City: Improvement Era, 1953], p. 459)

> One good yardstick as to whether a person might be the right one for you is this: in her presence, do you think your noblest thoughts, do you aspire to your finest deeds, do you wish

you were better than you are? (Ezra Taft Benson, "To the Single Adult Brethren of the Church," *Ensign*, May 1988, p. 53)

President McKay and President Benson have given us a fine definition of what *real* love feels like. Aside from the giddy high school feelings, real love makes you:

Feel a desire to achieve

Feel inspired to do your best

Want to make the most of yourself

Think your noblest thoughts

Aspire to your finest deeds

Wish you were better than you are

As you go through the courtship and engagement process, you'll often ponder the question, "Why do I love this person?" Among your list of reasons, I hope you will have these two: My fiancé is someone I *respect,* and my fiancé is someone I *admire.* Long after your youth and beauty have faded, those two qualities will still endure. They are at the core of real love. Someone that you respect and admire will no doubt create a similar response in others. And, speaking from experience, there is no greater thrill than to discover that those you admire and respect most, respect and admire your choice.

Many people die with their music still in them. Why is this so? Too often it is because they are always getting ready to live. Before they know it, time runs out.
—Oliver Wendell Holmes

I have spent my days stringing and unstringing my instrument, while the song I came to sing remains unsung.
—Tagore

WHAT TO DO WHILE YOU'RE WAITING

If I were you, what would I do, if courtship and marriage didn't come through? I'd fret, but I'd say there's not time to stew. Get busy, find something important to do.
—President Gordon B. Hinckley

YOU'D LIKE TO BE MARRIED, you hope and pray for it, but it isn't happening the way you planned. What do you do while you're waiting? Well, you sit on your hope chest and be miserable. Postpone all your plans and dreams, put all your eggs in the marriage basket, and wait for someone on a white horse to bring meaning to your life, right? Wrong!

You live your life in crescendo, that's what! You set aside the duet music for now, and you play what you can play! Play *loud*, play *well*, make *music!* Silent pianos do not attract crowds. Use all your talents and capacities to serve, learn, and grow. Remember, Nephi said, "I will go and do," not "I will sit and stew." God cannot steer a parked car, and we've got to be moving if we want him to guide us.

President Gordon B. Hinckley said:

> There are some who, for reasons unexplainable, do not have the opportunity of

marriage. To you I should like to say a word or two. Don't waste your time and wear out your lives wandering about in the wasteland of self-pity. God has given you talents of one kind or another. God has given you the capacity to serve the needs of others and bless their lives with your kindness and concern. Reach out to someone in need. There are so very many out there.

Add knowledge to knowledge. Refine your mind and skills in a chosen field of discipline. Never in the history of the world have women been afforded such opportunities in the professions, in business, in education, and in all of the honorable vocations of life. Do not feel that because you are single God has forsaken you. I repeat his promise quoted earlier, "Be thou humble; and the Lord thy God shall lead thee by the hand, and give thee answer to thy prayers." [D&C 112:10.]

The world needs you. The Church needs you. So very many people and causes need your strength and wisdom and talents. (*Teachings of Gordon B. Hinckley* [Salt Lake City: Deseret Book, 1997], pp. 601–2)

Get a Life!

Getting a life may be one of the first steps toward getting hitched. When I passed my mid-twenties as a single, one of my friends pointed out a statement he found in the March 1989 *Ensign*. (The entire issue is devoted to singles.) It helped me to see that waiting around for marriage to happen wasn't the best strategy. Elder John K. Carmack wrote:

> A large number of eternal marriage part-
> ners will find each other simply and naturally.
> . . . But what can be said about finding an eter-
> nal partner that will be helpful to those of you
> who are already in your late twenties, thirties,
> forties or beyond? . . . Marriage is more likely
> achieved as a by-product of pursuing other
> useful activities and goals. If I were single and
> had no prospects for marriage, after a reason-
> able time in one location and a careful weigh-
> ing of my job opportunities, I would probably
> explore other possibilities that could open new
> vistas for friendships and growth. But while
> temple marriage and family life would be my
> ultimate goal, whether in this life or beyond, I
> would be careful not to make it my central
> focus. *Marriage is more likely to come naturally,*
> *from living life fully, than by a direct and pointed*
> *campaign to achieve that long-range goal.* ("To
> My Single Friends," *Ensign,* March 1989, pp.
> 28–29; emphasis added)

Be Happily Single!

Happily single? Some might question this statement and say, "Why, you're not supposed to be happy if you're single!" Of course you are. Happiness is a choice, whether you're married or single. And happily single people are more likely to become happily married people. Sister Karen Lynn Davidson said, "I have yet to see marriage, by itself, turn an unhappy person into a happy person. A really happy married person is almost always one who was or could have been happy as a single person" (*Thriving on Our Differences* [Salt Lake City: Deseret Book, 1990], p. 39).

When we base our happiness on external things, we give our happiness to forces over which we have no control. Waiting for everything "out there" to be perfect before we can be happy will only lead to disappointment. An old Chinese proverb states, "He who waits for roast duck to fly into mouth must wait a long time." I don't know about you, but I've never seen a flock of roast ducks circling overhead. The only birds I know of that circle overhead are vultures. And they're more interested in eating you than in being eaten. Make sure those buzzards can tell the living from the dead—look alive!

At one time in my life, after a difficult breakup, I spent many weeks vegetating and feeling sorry for myself. I was sleeping in, moping around, going to work each day, but not really going anywhere. I finally got to the point where I was sick and tired of being sick and tired (an important point to get to when recovering from a heartbreak), when I stumbled across a statement made by President Hinckley. This quote was just what I needed. It thoroughly staggered me. It lifted me up, slammed me against the wall, threw cold water in my face, and pushed me back into life. (Pretty good for a bunch of words.) In fact, I liked it so much that I programmed my boom-box to play this quote each morning at 5:00 A.M. For the next few months, President Hinckley's words became my wake-up call to get my sorry, moping, self-absorbed tabernacle of clay out of bed in the morning and working on my new goals and my new purpose:

> One of the great tragedies we witness almost daily is the tragedy of men of high aim and low achievement. Their motives are noble. Their proclaimed ambition is praiseworthy. Their capacity is great. But their discipline is weak. They succumb to indolence. Appetite robs them of will. (*Be Thou an Example* [Salt Lake City: Deseret Book, 1981], p. 60)

If I have the chance to meet President Hinckley in the next life, I don't want him to look me over and say, "What a tragedy. He had high aim, but low achievement. He had great capacity, but he was lazy. His appetite for sleep and ease robbed his will." Up to this point, I'd been behaving like Purina Vulture Chow. Now I had to get out of bed and get to work. Perhaps you've heard it said, "Some people dream of doing great things; others wake up and do them." I had to wake up. Being single is no reason to be idle. I believe that the Lord will require us to make something of our lives whether we are married or not.

Find a Purpose!

I think some of the most attractive traits a person can have are a happy disposition, a good dose of appropriate self-confidence, and a sense of purpose. Earlier, we quoted the Prophet Joseph Smith, who from the confines of Liberty Jail told the Saints to cheerfully do all things that lay in their power. Now let's read the verse that comes right before. This is Doctrine and Covenants

123:16: "You know, brethren, that a very large ship is benefited very much by a very small helm in the time of a storm, by being kept workways with the wind and the waves."

What a wonderful concept! A ship without a rudder is tossed to and fro. Without a rudder, it has no direction, no course, no destination. If we're not careful, we may find ourselves being tossed about like a rudderless ship.

How do you weather the storm? Get yourself a purpose, a course, a destination! Find something to learn, someone to serve, and a new place to grow. This is what makes life meaningful and fulfilling.

Something to learn: If you spend an hour a day in your commute, that's about 260 hours per year on the road. If you listen only to the radio while you're driving, at the end of a year, what do you have to show for it? Anything? Instead, what if you went to your local bookstore or library and returned with an armful of informational or inspirational books or seminars on tape? How would you change and grow in one year if you listened to 260 hours of instruction and inspiration? You could become an expert in your field. You could learn another language. You could feed your spirit. Turn your car into a classroom to educate your mind and broaden your horizons. I've done this, and now I almost look forward to long drives. At times, I get so engrossed in the program I'm listening to, I drive right past my exit.

One of the best things I did during my single years was read books and listen to tapes on marriage. (You can't be too conspicuous, of course.) I learned so much about what makes good marriages work that it changed why I dated, how I dated, and even whom I dated. It also helped me avoid many of the problems common during the first year of marriage, because I was better prepared.

Someone to serve: We would all like to make a difference to one special person, but if that's not happening for you right now, you can find a way to make a difference to many other people. There are lonely people all over the world who need to be talked to or listened to. Hospitals and nursing homes love to have volunteers spend time with their patients. Your bishop may know of people in your own area who need assistance. Your extended family needs you too. You can become a world-class uncle, aunt, grandson, or granddaughter. There's nothing more uplifting than the feeling that you made a difference in someone's life.

On the other hand, nothing leads to discouragement more than sitting around doing nothing, waiting for your ship to come in. Elder Marion D. Hanks said: "At the moment of depression, if you will follow a simple program, you will get out of it. Get on your knees and get the help of God, then get up and go find somebody who needs something that you can help them with. Then it will be a good day" (Address given at Brigham Young University, September 27, 1966).

A new place to grow: Get out of your comfort zone and try something new. Not only will it make your life interesting but it will make you more interesting too. And you might even meet some interesting people. Maxwell Maltz suggested that "People who say that life is not worthwhile are really saying that they themselves have no personal goals which are worthwhile. . . . Get yourself a goal worth working for. Better still, get yourself a project. . . . Always have something ahead of you to 'look forward to'—to work for and hope for" (*The Best of Success,* comp. Wynn Davis [Lombard, Ill.: Celebrating Excellence, Inc., 1992], p. 208).

Tackle a project that gives you a reason to wake up each morning. When I was sixteen years old, I decided I wanted to write a book about making it through high school. Many years later, following a difficult breakup, I finally decided to get it done. I traded my least productive hours, 10:00 P.M. to midnight, for my most productive hours, 6:00 to 8:00 A.M. In other words, I went to bed at 10:00 P.M. and woke up at 5:00 A.M. (with a little help from President Hinckley). It worked! From 5:00 to 6:00 I showered, read my scriptures, and ate. Then I had two hours I never thought I had. From 6:00 to 8:00 I worked without interruption. It's amazing how nobody calls you or comes to see you between 6:00 and 8:00 A.M.

I wrote as much as I could each morning, and I found that this was one of the happiest times of my life. When someone asked me, "What are you doing these days?" it was really fun to say, "I'm writing a book." Although I spent the vast majority of time working at my full-time job and doing other things, those two little hours in the morning defined my day and my life. They broke my routine and eliminated my depression.

What could you accomplish if you found two hours each day? Certainly you've got a project or a goal somewhere in the back of your head, haven't you? Imagine how much you could do in just one month on the two-hours-a-day plan. Imagine how you could learn and grow and develop new talents. Letterman and Leno will just have to do without you. You've got better things to do. Doesn't the idea make you a little bit excited?

Trust the Lord

There are times in our lives when the only thing we can rely on is our testimony. We can't understand why things happen the way they do, but we know that the Lord loves us. Knowing that he really loves us is helpful when we don't understand the rest. Nephi said to the angel, "I know that [God] loveth his children; nevertheless, I do not know the meaning of all things" (1 Nephi 11:17). Whether we marry in this life or not, we have been told that the Lord will reward our love and faithfulness with blessings beyond our comprehension. Paul tells us that "Eye hath not seen, nor ear heard, neither have entered into the heart of man, the things which God hath prepared for them that love him" (1 Corinthians 2:9).

Trusting the Lord may also mean trusting his timing. Many times, as a young single adult, I would reflect on Doctrine and Covenants 111:11: "Therefore, be ye as wise as serpents and yet without sin; and I will order all things for your good, as fast as ye are able to receive them."

Remember that we will be judged according to our desires. The fact that you *desire* marriage may be more important than you realize. Listen to this story from President Boyd K. Packer:

> Some years ago a president of a student stake asked if I would counsel with a young

couple. The stalwart young man and his lovely wife had recently been told, with some finality, that they would never have children of their own. They were heartbroken as they sobbed out their disappointment. What they wanted most in life, what they had been taught and knew was an obligation and a privilege beyond price . . . they now were to be denied. Why? Why? Why?

I consoled them as best I could and offered comfort that really was insufficient to quiet the pain they felt. As they were leaving the office, I called them back and said: "You are a very fortunate and very blessed young couple."

They were startled, and the young man asked why I would say such a thing as that. Did I not understand what they had told me? Why would I say they were fortunate and blessed, when they were to be denied the thing they wanted most, children of their own?

I answered, "Because you *want* them. In the eternal scheme of things that will be of inestimable and eternal value." The Lord has said that he "will judge all men according to their works; according to the desire of their hearts" (D&C 137:9). ("The Play and the Plan," Church Educational System Fireside, May 7, 1995)

King Benjamin taught his people the importance of their desires: "I would that ye would say in your hearts that: I give not because I have not, but if I had I would give" (Mosiah 4:24). Similarly, we can say in our hearts that we would like to be married if we were capable of making it happen on our own.

Sometimes the only thing you can do is rely on the knowledge that the Lord knows your heart and knows how hard you are trying. Even if you and the Lord are the only ones who know your true desires, you're the only two that matter.

It's difficult. When you're single, some people believe that with a few carefully worded questions they can figure out exactly what your "problem" is—even though you've been fasting and praying and stewing and pondering about it for years. When people sometimes approach your piano and make careless assumptions, be careful. Don't let yourself become bitter. Just remember that you and the Lord know the real truth. Play what you can play and keep trying.

There are many things in life that on the surface don't seem to make sense. One single adult woman whom I greatly admire and respect told me that if prayer and fasting and visiting the temple were all that were required for finding a husband, she would have Nephis lined up at her door. Sometimes you can do everything you're supposed to and still not receive the desired blessing. Nephi did everything he was supposed to without murmuring and yet received horrible treatment from his brothers. Abinadi died an awful death although he did everything he was asked. And, of course, Jesus lived a perfect life and suffered more than man could suffer. Countless other examples could be offered, but suffice it to say, living right does not necessarily mean living easily. I have been touched by the words of this poem:

131

My life is but a weaving between
    my God and me.
I do not choose the colors; He worketh
    steadily.
Ofttimes He weaveth sorrow, and I
    in foolish pride
Forget He sees the upper and I the underside.

Not till the loom is silent, and shuttles
    cease to fly,
Will God unroll the canvas and explain
    the reason why
The dark threads are as needful in the
    skillful Weaver's hand
As the threads of gold and silver in the
    pattern He has planned.
("The Weaver," in Book of Poetry, ed. Al
    Bryant [New York: Zondervan Publishing
    House, 1968])

Single or married, what we are all really searching for
is peace. Peace is the feeling that we are doing the best
we can with what we have. Peace is the feeling that we
could face God and be comfortable with his knowing
the desires of our hearts. Peace is knowing that one day,
God will "explain the reasons why." To find real peace,
we must turn to the Prince of peace. Jesus taught, "Peace
I leave with you, my peace I give unto you: not as the
world giveth, give I unto you. Let not your heart be
troubled, neither let it be afraid" (John 14:27).

I've read this verse many times in the past, but I had
never thought of it as a commandment until I heard a

talk by Elder Jeffrey R. Holland. Speaking of this scripture, he said:

> I submit to you, that this may be one of the Savior's commandments that is, even in the hearts of otherwise faithful Latter-day Saints, almost universally disobeyed. . . . I am convinced that none of us can appreciate how deeply it wounds the loving heart of the Savior of the world, when he finds that his people do not feel confident in his care or secure in his hands or trust in his commandments. ("Come Unto Me," Church Educational System Fireside, March 2, 1997.)

Bottom line: You can trust Him. So you do what you can do, and find peace in the Savior.

Closing Thoughts

The title of this book is *What I Wish I'd Known When I Was Single.* The "I" pronoun appears three times in that title. That's a little embarrassing. But it is accurate. I can only write about *my own* brainlessness, or about what I wish *I* had known, which means this book isn't perfect. Maybe the things you needed weren't here. If that's the case, I apologize. But I know where the answers can be found, and so do you.

Many years ago, when Albert Einstein was teaching physics at Princeton, his graduate assistant noticed that Dr. Einstein gave the same midterm exam to his students two years in a row. When the assistant asked why, Dr. Einstein explained, "Since last year, the answers have changed." When it comes to the sciences and the philosophies of men, the answers change—sometimes annually. But you and I know where to look for answers that never change. We have them in abundance, and they're found in the gospel. Once again, I'm grateful for the scriptures and the words of inspired leaders and teachers who have helped me and will continue to help me find the answers that don't change.

So what would I recommend, if you're entering the world of young single adults? First of all, I would have a plan for my life: mission, education, the works. (As you know, the best way to predict your success in life is to create it, and you create it with a plan.) I would set my goals high concerning my education and my own spiritual development, but I would be careful not to focus on the things I couldn't control. Then I would live my life at the top of my lungs. I would worry less and laugh more. I would try new things and experience life to the fullest. I wouldn't wait for this goal or that goal to be achieved before I could be happy. I would face each day full of hope and faith. I wouldn't let the little things get me down.

And when it comes to relationships, I would spend less money on extravagant dates at nice restaurants and spend more time talking and sharing ideas. I would focus less on trying to find someone and more on trying to become someone. I would be careful with the feelings of others in my words and expressions of affection. I would try not to let breakups break me up. I would never give up on dating, but I would give up on worrying and stewing about it. When people approached my piano with their advice, I would smile and say, "I'm doing my best."

I would take the Lord at his word when he said, "Let

not your heart be troubled, neither let it be afraid." I would realize that a happy disposition and a quiet self-assurance that come from a heart full of faith and hope are more attractive than a disposition of doubt, cynicism, bitterness, and fear. (In fact, a quiet confidence in God's promises is infinitely more attractive than muscles and a Jeep.)

Whatever difficulties came my way, I would rely on my anchors and keep the faith. I would remember that I have a Father in Heaven who loves me, and I would trust him to order all things for my good. I would realize that there are lessons to be learned from trials as well as triumphs, and I would welcome every opportunity life offered me for growth and experience.

Finally, I would be committed to making a difference in the lives of others. I would realize that wealth, fame, and position are empty pursuits, while forgetting ourselves in service is where we'll find ourselves. The Savior has commanded all people, both married and single, to love one another as he has loved us. So whether I was alone or in a duet, I would find a way to make sure that my life meant something. I would want the world to be a better place because I was here.

Well, this little book is done. As a young single adult, I looked for information to help answer my questions. I found lots of great quotes and principles, and I tried to put all those answers under one cover. I'm sorry if it didn't answer all of your questions. But I firmly believe the answers we all need are out there, and they're found in the gospel. Best wishes in your searching! I hope to see you happily making music wherever you are.

INDEX